Past Immiscible: Digging into Uncommon Ground

John G. Sabol

Also by John Sabol...

Ghost Excavator (2007)
Ghost Culture (2007)
Gettysburg Unearthed (2007)
Battlefield Hauntscape (2008)
The Anthracite Coal Region (2008)
The Politics of Presence (2008)
Bodies of Substance, Fragments of Memory (2009)
Phantom Gettysburg (2009)
Digging Deep (2009)
The Re-Haunting(s) of Gettysburg (2010)
The Haunted Theatre (2011)
Ghost Culture Too (2012)
Beyond the Paranormal (2012)
Digging-Up Ghosts (2nd publishing, 2013)
Burnside Bridge (2013)
The Gettysburg Experience (2013)
The Absence Above, A Presence Below (2013)
The Production of Haunted Space (2013)
Centralia, Pennsylvania (2013)
The Ghost Excavation (2013)
The Good Death and the Civil War (2014)
Centralia: A Vision of Ruin (2014)
Altered States: Making the Extraordinary
Ordinary Again (2014)
Archaeology and Ghost Research: A Relational Entanglement (2014)
Performances in Haunted Space: An Afterlife in Ruin (2014)
Haunting Presences, Ruins, and Ghostly Entanglements (2015)
The Afterlife of Centralia: Presences in a Landscape of
Destruction (2015)
An Archaeology Without Borders: Performance Excavations in
Embedded/Entangled Fields (2016)
Ghost Hunt: Exploding the Myths/Exploring the Possibility (2016)
The Haunting of the Omni Bedford Springs Resort and Spa (2016)
The Haunting Presences of the Omni Bedford Springs (2017)
Victorian Ghosts of the Omni Bedford Springs:
Representation and Reveal (2017)
Walking the Ghostly Spaces of Bedford Springs:
The Movement of Presence (2017)

~John G. Sabol~

Past Immiscible:

Digging into Uncommon Ground

Ghost Excavator Books, Inc. ™©

Bedford, Pennsylvania,
USA

~John G. Sabol~

Preface:

'Excavating' Vulnerabilities

"Of course I've waited too long before writing this and now it is late…like beginning to write at twilight with no lamp as the darkness falls…But it is really dark now…and it is getting very late".

- Allon White, " To Close to the Bone: Fragments of an Autobiography" (1989)

As archaeologists, we must be sensitive to a past still becoming present, and to a sensible archaeology that breaks the code. Archaeologists must become vulnerable observer-participants to what still 'percolates' in archaeological space. A too-often hidden narrative, and lost experiential stories of archaeological fieldwork, must be excavated and exposed.

We must include those traces and fragments of durational sensory elements of the past long ignored in field notes and site reports. This stance, speaking about and writing an immiscible narrative entanglement of material culture and a 'percolating' sensorium, must begin.

I, myself, am guilty. For too long, I have failed to identify (even ignore) stories or accept experiences (even personal

~John G. Sabol~

3

ones) that occurred in the field. It was so because these encounters were not part of the training of, and acculturation to, the rite of passage of being an archaeologist: the 'archaeologiness' of fieldwork. These occurrences were not even part of the use of the "archaeological imagination", but something else still present, a duration that continued.

This is a book about the practice of archaeology. In particular, to use John Schofield's words, it is about "the practice that really defines our discipline and gives it public recognition and support: excavation" (2011:11). However, as pointed out in a recent book, Silliman (2018), "archaeology is way more than just digging" (2018:3). That approach is taken here: 'excavating' at times without actually physically 'digging'.

An excavation is like travel, but when most archaeologists reach the 'destination', no one is there to greet them, or show them what the place is (still) really like. Yet, on an excavation, one doesn't imagine these other worlds. There is material evidence, and one is confronted with it on an almost daily basis. But how far does one immerse into that other world(s)? How close does one stay within one's own cultural, professional, and disciplinary boundaries? Does memory remain embedded to the present? How much of the 'subject' of one's inquiries is lost where one still remains 'attached' in an 'etic' position? Sir Mortimer Wheeler, more than six decades ago (1954), said that "there is no one right way of digging, but there are many wrong ways". Hopefully, what follows is not perceived as an orientation of one of those 'wrong ways'. Archaeological fieldwork is fascinating, bizarre, uncanny, and disturbing. An archaeological excavation is a potential point of access to an infinite number of worldviews and layers of memory. The archaeological universe of survey and excavation, to use Graham Harman's concept of speculative realist ontology,

"resembles a massive complex made up of numerous caverns, outer walls, alleyways, ladders, and subway systems, each sealed off from the others and defining its own space, but with points of access or passage filled with candles and searchlights that cast shadows into the next" (2005:233).

That archaeological world is composed of a wild and uncanny variety of arrangements and mutual disconnectivities of material and sensual presences. But there are lines of movement into this meshwork of exploration, as multiple pasts bleed into one another's realities. Archaeological fieldwork is this movement, serving both as a journey and a bridge to these other realities of past presence presenting in the present. Archaeology allows us to enter into "terrains of experience and knowledge which otherwise would be denied to us" (Strathern 1993:129).

The metaphor of the journey and the bridge, as Andrew Strathern says, "implies that serious gaps exist and that the bridges have to be constructed carefully or else they will break. It implies, too, that we want to cross over. And finally it suggests that if we make such a bridge, then in certain cases the movement across it can be reciprocal" (Ibid: 129).

This is a necessary 'witnessing' for archaeologists, but how much of the present changes these pasts on the journey at the edge of a trowel? How much more is there, at the edge of a 'percolating' presence? It is well known that excavation is a destructive process. Less focus, however, centers on the destruction of the archaeological experience.

Sensual, non-visual perception is difficult among the strata of ruinous archaeological records, where multiple slices of percolating sensual temporalities float around, as they intersect within one another's sensuous fields.   One's interactions on site (and in the 'trenches'), working with what remains cannot be exactly reproduced. Some encounters are unique, irrecoverable, the ephemerality of some presences means that they are gone as they happen, always occurring in the present, and seldom recorded (these uncanny, ephemeral moments)as a future tense in site reports.

What happened to the narrative of the past in these instances? Is this experience documented? Why not? Is it because "we lack the language to articulate what takes place when we are in fact at work" (Geertz 1995:44)? How do we bring that particular archaeological moment back? How do we unearth it again?

How do we communicate that 'close encounter', when the distance of past presence melts before our senses and our archaeological rationality? How do we represent it? Can we? Should we? Will it become a theatricality of farce if we speak about it, or record it in an archaeological narrative? Are we so vulnerable (or not enough) to such intimacy and subjectivity to these surface percolations? Does it make us become too personal when working with what remains of the past?

I want to expose a relation here – and not the present to the past – but one between the archaeologist as observer and the sensed exposure of oneself as a spectator to a place from the past (or its embedded memories). We seldom venture towards these memories when we excavate. This is because it is not part of our training and enculturation into 'archaeologiness'.

I want to make my emotions part of my archaeological work, and extend them as I work with these percolating presences of the past. I want my sense of emplacement, my position in the excavation process, to replace the professional rituals of archaeological displacement within the tropes of 'archaeologiness'.

In the field, as presences of the past move toward us, I don't want to step back and be objective. I don't want to move aside and forget what just happened. I don't want a part of the past to become lost because of my conscious inability to act. I don't want to leave behind a trail of destruction and erasures without production, inscribing something new rather than affording opportunities for the past to become present. I want to create unfulfilled expectations upon those (both past and present) whom I study. I want that presence to continue, unabated, and address it socially.

Doing archaeology is not about creating a new and different archaeological record than that what is past and present today. As Sandra Harding (1987) has said:

"The beliefs and behaviors of the researcher are part of the empirical evidence for (or against) the claims advanced in the results of research".

I don't want that evidence to be strictly an 'etic' one. I also want an 'emic' presence to be sensed, experienced, and documented. So let's begin to 'excavate' anew, before the 'shadow' changes:

"There is a shadow on the wall before me. It is my own; the hour is late. I write in a hotel room at midnight. Tomorrow the shadow on the wall will be that of another".

- Loren Eiseley (*The Night Country,* 1971)

~John G. Sabol~

Introduction:

How Past is the Archaeological Present?

How familiar is the archaeological present? Is excavation grounded (either by experience or 'habit memory') in this familiarity, as researched and etic-based? How different might archaeology understand itself, and its passion the present past, if this familiarity becomes 'uncommon' ground? Can it conceive itself less as the 'digging' into material things and features, the unearthing of buried humanity, and more as an open-ended, performative exploration of alternative possibilities: new ways of a past becoming present, an 'other' sense of being and becoming present? It is said that archaeology is memory work, but whose buried memory is it? Are archaeologists not revealing all of the past, as it is encountered and experienced? Does it merely reveal an archaeology as 'habit memory'?

Alfredo Gonzalez-Ruibal (2013) has said this:

"the idea of the archaeological excavation has focused too restrictively on a few issues, such as acts of discovery, unearthing and reconstructing the past and the multi-layered nature of the archaeological record. This leaves

~John G. Sabol~

9

aside…many other things that happen in archaeological excavations" (2013:7).

If "something of the essence of archaeology (is) really bound up with excavation" (Edgeworth 2011:44), then how we perform that excavation can alter our experience of the archaeological record.

Excavation, in its broadest use as an experiential tool, must become more than a silent (sense(less) witness incapable of (or indifferent to) 'triggering' what else remains of the present past. Is reconstructing the past and its physical remains merely representations that oft times become a sort of fiction that passes for fact for the spurious purpose of providing the public with pleasure (cf. Hewison 1989), not real presence?

 If "clearing the ground" is a "crucial rite of passage for archaeologists" (Ibid: 45) to become archaeologists, then this rite of passage, which includes all fieldwork operational 'rituals', involves theatrical performativity. This is the rite that transforms one to an archaeologist who practices "archaeologiness" (cf. Gnecco 2013). Do archaeologists merely "become part of the guild only by learning where and how to dig"? Is "the experience of fieldwork (utterly legitimized by digging)"? Is this "the ultimate place, source, and locus of archaeologiness - the sense of being an archaeologist" (Ibid: 69)?

Within this 'archaeologiness', the discipline of archaeology is a series of linked metaphors: "excavation, stratigraphy, typology, discovery, and search for origins" (Harrison 2013:46). Do archaeologists take for granted these metaphors, a cog in the machine that interprets the past? The majority of these metaphors relate to a perception of vision as the paradigmatic frame. Do we, how do we, separate the other senses from that metaphoric vision? How authentic and meaningful, even representative, is that past record based on the use of these metaphors?

Are the worlds encountered in the field mostly inhabited by understanding models of the past designed by enculturated archaeologists who conform to this archaeological pattern of metaphoric 'archaeologiness'?? Is this 'ethnographic reality'? "Who' or what becomes present in an excavated space of shared experiences between different worlds, not contemporary past ones? Is this reality merely an experience that conforms to the habit memory of contemporary 'archaeologiness'? Anthropologist Michael Taussig has said that "all societies live by fictions taken as real" (1987:121). Do archaeologists, as a disciplinary 'guild', live by the fiction of 'archaeologiness'? Do they follow a certain etic-inspired path in fieldwork, interpreting at the trowel's edge, yet out of the grasp of experiencing the past as it emerges in other sensorial forms of life?

Greg Dening (1996) suggests that "relics of the past cross all the cultural boundaries that lie between past and present, and when they do, they are reconstituted in the relations and means of production of each cultural zone they enter" (1996:43). Has the 'times' of various archaeological theories and methodologies still producing merely 'tricks of the trade', rather than emically-sound (alternative) versions of the archaeological record? Today, as in the past, are these 'cultural zones' in large measure merely archaeological (not ethnographically) sensitive and sensible?

Coll Thrush, a historian, in a paper (2011) about "Hauntings as Histories", raises a set of questions for archaeologists: "Do nonliving (or nonhuman) forces have agency?" "Is the past even really past?" More significant questions he asks: "Can a single place be home to a certain kind of history, persistent and cohesive, even across boundaries of time and cultural regime?" "Can remnants of past societies – ruins, ecological footprints, artifacts – 'speak' in active ways for the histories they represent?" (2011:54). The idea that sites have "both identity and agency" is central to an emic perspective.

The idea of an emic perspective, however, is framed by a number of 'spirited' questionings: can archaeological survey reach the dead? Do excavations? As we unbound objects and presences from where they were, does this disturb the dead? As environmental conditions alter the settings of past occupations, how does this affect possible attached past presence? As archaeologists, can we look at the ontological status of 'spirits' and their involvement with materiality in the archaeological record?

Is there archaeological data of 'ontological shifts'? Can we link ontology and materiality? Such a linkage would "take 'things' encountered in the field as they present themselves, rather than immediately assuming that they signify, represent, or stand for something else" (Henare, Holbraad, and Wastell 2007:2).

In a recent paper, Vesa-Pekka Herva (2014) takes up this issue when she analyses the material heritage associated with Second World War German culture remaining in Finnish Lapland from a haunting perspective. The paper "draws on recent research and thinking on ghosts and hauntings, modern ruins and theoretically-informed approaches to material culture" (2014:298).

According to Herva, "military equipment would have "abducted" (Gell 1998) qualities of the German army...and are still more or less residually charged by those qualities" (Ibid: 306). They are not considered dead matter or "matter out of place" (Douglas 1966:36). Thus, something of the German presence, besides their material culture, remains. It "haunts the present not just metaphorically but also in a more literal sense" (Herva 2014:308).

As an "extension of perceiving" (Gibson 1986:258), the coupled system of material and presence "provides new possibilities for perceiving, thinking, and acting" (Herva 2014:309) beyond the traditional archaeological tropes and the enculturation process into 'archaeologiness'. It creates an archaeological reality beyond the physical remains of the archaeological gaze.

Are ruins, in general, kinds of special places that form affordances for various sensory and bodily experiences, ones that archaeologists encounter, but seldom publicly acknowledge? Are such unacknowledged absent presences in archaeological field reports examples of Graves-Brown (2011) observation that "the habitual tropes of archaeological practice either do not work, or need to be rethought and reconfigured" (2011:168)?

Do such 'percolating', past presences, those with an agentic capacity, create a transformative potential in the constitution of both present and future archaeological realities? Are these traces or fragments of past worlds (as individual or collective memories) surfacing mixed together? Do they represent pasts that are still in production? Whatever their contemporary perceived meaning among archaeologists, they certainly are more than the surface of the present an excavation usually exposes.

What about bones as materiality, and their relation to a 'spectral turn' in archaeological fieldwork? Bones are the most intimate of all ruins (cf. Ginsberg 2004:407). The universality of hauntings and ghost stories associated with bones all over the world attest to the uncanny, affording power of their unearthing during archaeological fieldwork.

Gregory Delaplace (2014) has proposed a notion he calls "regimes of communicability". One way to take these manifestations (as percolating, ephemeral presences), and ontology, seriously is to analyze under which circumstances they appear to which people, in specific ways, at a certain time. Do they manifest during archaeological excavations, especially when unearthing material objects and/or burials?

Is archaeological excavation a 'regime of communicability' that can afford an 'active' (or 'activate') a particular 'form of life' of the presence of the past today? From "a methodological point of view" are these manifesting sensorial elements in motion something that can "illuminate their human and social context" (cf. Appadurai 1986:5)?

The main archaeological metaphors, mentioned by Harrison (2013), afford restrictions, a characteristic human trait:

"One does what one's time dictates does one not? One does what one is ordered or expected to do, not necessarily because one is a coward, but because one is a trained, conditioned professional. A soldier, really. The unexpected event, if it ever comes, leaves one unprepared and fumbling" (Eiseley 1975:100).

Archaeologists, while stressing academic rigor and the social creation of knowledge, must confront their past (and present) self-imposed limitations. This is no easy task:

"What regularly happens in the struggle to express our findings is that we bend the accepted meaning of terms in our language of communication in order to encompass the senses of words in the language of investigation" (Strathern 1993:78).

We cannot, in a theoretical, practical, and economic sense excavate all of the layers of strata in the archaeological record of a site. As Loren Eiseley (1975) has said:

"as any archaeologist will tell you, there is never the means to unearth all the rooms, or follow the buried roads, or dig into every cistern for treasure. You try to see what the ruin meant to whoever inhabited it and, if you are lucky, you see a little way backward into time" (1975:217).

In the meantime, the question remains: are we, the archaeologists, the trickster, fooling ourselves and others?

Every archaeologist must 'excavate' their own role in this relation to what remains of the past, their own core concepts of 'archaeologiness' which tend to structure the 'usual suspects' in how sites are selected, experienced, and interpreted. Does this 'archaeologiness' become more important than knowledge and skill. Sometimes, it does:

"Many people join, or are selected for projects, and return year after year to the same excavations, not because of their knowledge or skill with respect to the project's archaeology, but because they are contributors to, and willing participants in the conditions and collective character of the project" (Bender et.al. 2007:66).

Archaeological excavation is a form of place making. Excavation is action. This action puts fieldwork in place "in the realm of cultural meaning-making, performance, and communicative practice" (DeLoria 2006:16). The social practices involved in constructing a site's occupational record, not re-constructing a past presence, inscribes contemporary memories that can erase some of the experiences of past occupations. Place, as 'host' is altered.

 Further, what is made known to 'outsiders' has frequently excluded experiences, devalued certain uncanny presences, and erased actors. Is excavation, then, really creative place making? Is there a sensitivity toward the recovery of subtle, percolating, uncanny elements that hint at continuities of 'active' presence?

Bettina Arnold (1999) has said this: "The archaeological past is perceived as passive, fixed in time and place precisely because it is 'past'" (1999:1). This perception is based on giving too much priority to a limited number of entities, at the expense of others. Emerging, uncanny presences can cause surprise, contradiction, and all too often ignored.

But do these uncanny, ephemeral appearances lead to a "historical schizophrenia" (Colwell-Chanthaphonb et.al. 2008:63)? They do "if the expectation is that archaeological inquiry must lead to a single truth, a single understanding of the past" (Ibid: 63).

If "the present…reproduces itself in the form of the past" (Morphy 1993:239-240), then all forms of percolating presences warrant our attention. Archaeological landscapes, like cultural landscapes, provide a means to unite the past and the present in a personal experience (cf. Kuchler 1993). But does it do this thru the excavation process?

~John G. Sabol~

If the archaeological record is a 'thick' place, "suffused with a sense of sensual, emotional, and affective belonging that is embedded over time through repetitive, practical, embodied engagement" (Edensor 2012:1106), why, then, are most archaeological reports 'thin' descriptions, seldom involving sensual, emotional, and affective modalities?

Jacques Derrida (1994) describes 'spectres' as that which history has suppressed. He labels this a 'hauntology', an account of absent presences and 'spectral' remains. Is the 'rite of passage' of 'archaeologiness' contributing to a 'hauntology' of missing pieces in a site's archaeological record? Is the 'technology' of excavation inadequate for unearthing bodies of memory and past performances that may still be attached (or embedded) in the archaeological record?

We must unbound a site, as that archaeological place, destabilize its (exclusive) claim to the past, move toward a contemporary "authentic character" with no "single unique identities" (Massey 1994:155). This opens a dig by creating a multiplicity of presence and time dimensions, within an entanglement of different agents, actants, affordances, and agencies.

It means, in an archaeological sense, that a site or landscape is "never finished or complete, not easily framed or read" (Cresswell 2003:280). Finally, the presence of the archaeologist in the archaeological record during the excavation process, adds to the mix of a co-mingled and coequal past/present. The site/landscape becomes a series of "porous networks of social relations" (Ibid: 121).

Seamus Heaney, the celebrated Irish poet, once said: "We can all live in two or three places at the same time". Archaeological fieldwork is an example of this. It includes contemporary excavation space, immersive performance practices, as a reaction to the presence of the past during excavation, and the use of the archaeological imagination as part of the experience. Too often, however, these elements merge to create the 'habit memory' of 'archaeologiness', resulting in the 'black holes' of fieldwork. Jon Stallworthy (1982) noted that "the spade...descends into darkness to bring what is buried to the light". But is the spade (or the trowel) the only means to illuminate the past in the present?

What happens when the unexpected (or the 'uncanny') occurs? What occurs when a re-emergence, not quite familiar, presents itself? Do certain uncanny returns of the past create a breach within the standard tropes of archaeological work? What happens when what remains of the past in the present do not remain rooted to stratigraphy, 'buried' history, and archaeological knowledge? Can we draw inferences from uncanny traces that present themselves in sometimes unfamiliar episodes of fieldwork?

Do we, can we, re-connect during survey and/or excavation (not simply 'unearth' material remains) to a 'live' or still forming past that remains present?

~John G. Sabol~

19

"A repeated gesture, an aged object…a footprint…all of these things, material and immaterial might drag something of the no longer now into the present, or drag the present into the no longer now" (Schneider 2014:45).

We need to become more sensorial attentive to how fieldwork can affect us, and to the emotional ecologies that still remain embedded and attached in layers of memory in the archaeological record. Can this affect be more than a residual ephemeral moment? Can it be sociable? That liminal state, between attention to material detail and attentive to percolating sensorial ephemeral ties, can change to transformations in the archaeological record and the affording position of the archaeologist.

This type of relational ontology, the co-presence of then and now in a relational entanglement (cf. Watts 2013) "can open…to new worlds of understanding between what is meant to be…a human person versus a non-human person, and even alive vs. dead" (McNiven 2013). Do such encounters challenge us as archaeologists, or do we merely ignore their ephemeral presences? The present we sometimes experience is very much a continuing production of this 'lively' past. Through percolating trace elements, the past has not left us. These are traces of remains that should capture our attention and interest. Mostly, they don't. They should prompt us to reflect and explore directions other than those commonly followed by the tropes of survey and excavation. These are affording memories, social in nature, that move through several

~John G. Sabol~

temporalities simultaneously. What was, what still is, what continues to endure must be deposited into our archaeological agendas as something beyond 'mind prints' to our conversations during non-academic social interactions.

An archaeology that immerses itself within this presence of the present must take responsibility and show respect when looking back (not down), trying to sense that particular 'form of life' from a different position, one of equality not authority. It is taking a sense-able stance. To do this, we must re-think the significance of survey and excavation as social nearness, not material distance from these attachments of presence. Archaeology considers as properly archaeological only the moment when the excavator "identifies a contact in the ground, and dissolves that very contact by virtue of observing and recording it" (Buccellati 2017:1).

Whether this contact is through technology or the trowel, it is a physical, visual 'nearness', not a social proximity to the presence of the past. But is this the only archaeological moment, the 'dig' contact of observation? Are there secondary moments, beyond time constraints, that are also properly archaeological? Are there other movements, other roots and routes, toward the past becoming an engagement with a present reality? Can the archaeologist become a contemporary ethnographic 'witness' of a trace of past cultural expression becoming present?

~John G. Sabol~

Is an archaeological site a record of perspectivism in which spaces of the landscape are "inhabited by different sorts of subjects or persons, human and non-human, which apprehend reality from distinct points of view" (Viveiros de Castro 1998:469)? In this archaeological perspectivism, as 'excavating' performance practices as one simulates another's bodily behavior, senses, and sensibility empathetically, acquiring a sense of past reality in a form of "mimetic empathy" (Willerslev 2007:106)? Can this afford a sensitivity to the perspective of the other, perhaps "the closest one can come to experiencing another's point of view without being that other in an absolute sense" (Ibid: 107)?

This archaeological approach becomes a means to being bound up together in a relational way during excavation in a specific rhythmic context, perhaps as a result of a trace or fragment of the past becoming present. This process can be viewed as a transduction from one medium (physical excavation) to another, a social behavior, context-specific to a particular space/time dimension. Thus, interpretation and meaning occurs, not specifically at "the trowel's edge", but primarily constituted in socially-affording rhythmic performance practices that target context-specific layers of possible attached memories.

Archaeological fieldwork is mostly about eroding the ruin, its otherness, and rendering it familiar through a reconstruction of what materially remains. In practice and practical terms, archaeology is about converting the trace and fragmented archaeological, instead of experiencing what persists behind the ruin, the trace, the fragment, and the experience of excavating past spaces. Archaeology is not about the presence of the past, but rather about what archaeologists assume it to be. This assumption is based on a concept of a ruination of presence.

What other presences that may be accessible is based on our contemporary performance practices. That accessibility is based on deconstructing reconstruction, and the tradition-bound 'archaeologiness' of archaeology. Most existing conceptual schemes deny the possibility that there is anything beyond the material trace, the fragmented assemblage or structure, the ruin. There is no follow through between the narrative produced and all the phenomena observed and sensed. Description relies on a particular way of seeing, even imagining, and way of thinking. This is derived, in large part, from the 'habit memories' of survey and excavation.

There is clearly more to the contemporary archaeological record than the vertical surface of the present that is usually exposed through excavations into the 'darkness' cited by Jon Stallworthy (1982). This means that interpretations at the trowel's edge can become a limiting means (as a 'habit memory') of understanding the archaeological present. The interpretive process is active and must be contingent upon a relationality between object and objectives, between subject and subjective experience, and between the liminal

~John G. Sabol~

space of contact and the performance practices that can transform the contemporary archaeological record.

Archaeology has much to gain by experimenting with various performance and experience-based approaches that may document other dynamically-relational 'living' material/immaterial assemblages and sensory ephemeral ties. All excavation exposures should be baselines for continuing intervention. Most, however, are premature ends due to various academic, social, and political constraints. We might follow Michael Shank's advice (1992) that a course in "sensuous receptivity" should be part of archaeological training (1992:192).

Such training could provide a means to effect various forms of social affordance, as it affects the re-occupation (as fieldwork) of sites surveyed and excavated by archaeologists. It also creates a different ritual process and activity sets, as a new rite of passage toward archaeological relations with what containments still remain embedded and attached to the archaeological present. The concept of sensuous fieldwork, as an active 'live' archaeology, makes ethnographic sense. It considers changes (as entanglements not separation) of state, as stages of receptivity to a present past. It uses the liminality of engaging archaeological space to rewrite parts of the 'surviving' record through the reincorporation into a different 'archaeologiness'. This becomes a form of experiencing the flow of mediations in a presence of the past that continues to become present.

~John G. Sabol~

In this alternative state of 'archaeologiness', the object (as a sensory culture) is not separated from its original context by time or physical processes. It remains, in situ, embedded and attached within" emotional and historical sedimentation" (Seremetakis 1996:7) or "sedimented layers of memory" (Tilley 1994:27). This creates a "growing fund for experience" (Casey 1987:284) during the excavation of the archaeological record. This is a particular articulation of the past erupting into the present. Such perceptions involve being open to how particular objects, artifact assemblages, and features of past occupations may still maintain a latent sensory agentic presence.

Fieldwork becomes a potential state as a liminal position in its relation to an ephemeral archaeological record. It incorporates (not ignores) a new status at sites (and in spaces) whose ephemeral memories had previously been silenced, through an active and conscious process (Connerton 2008) of academic strategies of "omitting memory" (Starzmann 2016:19) of certain materializing presences. Their reincorporation into the narratives of the archaeological record becomes an acceptance (a remembering) of these memories, not a rejection (a forgetting) of them. This is another form, I propose, of "engaging in archaeological ways of thinking about memory" (Starzmann and Roby 2016:3), by doing and experiencing.

The "centrality of digging" as the "essential spirit of the archaeological enterprise" (Edgeworth 2011:46) must involve 'emic' dimensions and include subjective experiences during fieldwork. This emic dimension, within the normally 'etic' habit memory of survey and excavation, is a re-envisioning of the concept of assemblage. It is a re-focus of its archaeological and social dimensions, consisting of a grouping (and relationality) of sensory elements and material remains, attached on the surface of exposure in the same archaeological context.

Socially, this affords a collection of contemporary human and non-human agents, and other embedded/attached presences, which all equally participate in the reality of the archaeological present (not past). This assemblage of objects, subjects, and experiences are "jumbled together in the present" (Harrison 2011:157). Archaeological intervention, experienced as a form of performance excavation, is a means of 'unearthing' something different from the habitual tropes of archaeological practices. This involves a direct experience with the intrusion of the past in the present as surfacing memories.

Such an assemblage relationality, between present and past performances, certainly has ontological implications in that it contributes to the re-shaping of the archaeological record, and that records' relation to time and memory. It creates an archaeological reality beyond what physically remains of the past. This transformative potential re-constitutes both the present and possible futures of particular archaeological records as an ongoing process of becoming a continuing future (not past) occupational profile.

We must think, inter-act (perform), and re-act (experience) to that presence becoming present from absence. To do this, we have to think of an excavation space that performs. Archaeological space is a performative medium, its record an inherently active entity. Archaeological space, during the excavation process, is an "event-space", a term attributed to contemporary architect Bernard Tschumi. Approaching space this way during excavation, the archaeological record becomes a series of layers of transitory events, creating a temporalization of space. This is characterized by movement (a percolating past becoming present), relativity (a context-specific relationality of affording and affecting behaviors), and duration (which includes episodes of ephemerality).

This results in a state of active materializations becoming the present, rather than a passive (and past) archaeological record. This is a result of actions in space (archaeologically-performing interventions) having an affording relationship within spaces of still attached presence. The archaeological space in excavation mode can be sensed and experienced as continuously fluctuating contemporary performances.

The ruin, or now 'empty', by the presence of the past surface landscape, as the site of excavation, is a particular mise-en-scene that becomes a mediated archaeological immersion that is normally 'out of time (and rhythm) within this archaeological record of percolating event-space. An excavation, as 'habit memory' of 'archaeologiness', is not designed to admit other worlds or realities. This is where the 'craft' of archaeological excavation enters into fieldwork. The event-space challenges us to 'craft', not how to dig, but rather excavating performance practices that target these emerging presences. The site (and spaces) of excavation must become an anti (past)-monument/present ruin space, as a temporally-bound spacial entity. This allows what else remains of multiple presences to pass through and become present.

Let's be sensible here. There is a fog hovering over our excavating spaces. It deadens perception. Data can no longer be considered solely as an extraction from the ground. Sometimes, knowledge is produced by determining the voice of acousmatic sounds, the sense of experience, the touch that reaches beyond the imagination, and the scent of something long considered dead. Following a call for a "poetic archaeology", Ian Russell (2006) suggests we become "less concerned with what an archaeology might be and more with what an archaeology might do" (2006:32). What is it that archaeologists might do, and why must archaeology do something else?

Mary Weismantle (2015:146) argues that there are multiple realities (in the contemporary archaeological record), and that this does transform social experience, especially during archaeological intervention, such as, I propose, the excavation process. This book examines the archaeological and the archaeological record through a focus on a continuing, percolating past. This past becoming present is both residual and agentic presence. These materializations represent active traces and fragments of past realities. This 'other' record forms part of a non-representationalist archaeology, transformations that can become present through particular performance practices during archaeological fieldwork:

"All past events are more remote from our senses than the stars of the remotest galaxies"

- George Kubler (1962)

That vision of the past cannot be an archaeological one today. We <u>can</u> 'sense' those remote galaxies, and today we can experience sensory traces of the past still becoming present. We cannot continue to allow archaeological field practices to form 'black holes' of absence!

What follows is my "turn" toward what archaeology might be, and why.

~John G. Sabol~

Table of Contents

Photographs

Winchester, UK

Cholula, Mexico

<u>What!</u>

The Archaeologist as Trickster

"I have been both excited about what the shovel would reveal and disconsolate and stricken at the sacrilege done to the dead".

- Loren Eiseley (1975:94)

Today, at a time when much archaeological thinking appears as dead as the perceived past it explores, is this lack of execution part of the craft of archaeologiness, or a trick of the archaeological enculturation process? Do we use the archaeological imagination to merely mold our artifact 'treats', rather than extend our sensory horizons back past the ground, and etic-grounded ideas in which we excavate?

How do we tell the story of the archaeological record? Does our craft enculturation sometimes trick us? The trickster in indigenous ontologies is about death and time, something archaeologists are well acquainted with. In the view of Pearson and Shanks (2001), archaeology is the science of ruins and the abandoned, of fragments and death (cf. 2001:91-93). It is a time of present absences. But this time is not somewhere 'out there'. It lies "buried (even when excavated) and hidden in the landscape" (Crang and Travlou 2001:170). It lies in exposed heterogeneous layers of contemporary disassociation, masking movements between the levels of physicality and memory, embedded and attached.

The ruin becomes a way of publicly inscribing and distinguishing an 'archaeological space', a space where archaeologiness, as a rite of passage, is performed and narrated, both through the ruin itself, and the 'ceremonies' of 'habit memory' (in survey and excavation) that takes place around it. But there is something more. The ruin and abandoned landscape carry a deeper memory of the past within its present form. These layers of deeper memory are not physically distant, but surfacing as becomings. They are surfaces of identity on the ground, presences present without trowel help.

"If the postmodern archaeologist searches for unusual archaeological locations, liminal sites which challenge the conventional distinctions between the surfaces and depths of the earth and do not fit the traditional concept of grounded excavation" (Wallace 2004:196), then the time is now to excavate without machinery, shovels, trowels....

What becomes of those stories edited from 'official' archaeological accounts of the past? Rather than consider archaeologists as storytellers, might we not consider some as the stories themselves: as a trickster belonging to, and part of, a 'secret story' that haunts the emerging presence of the past during fieldwork? Archaeology's story might be perceived, not as a linear sequence of site events or historical episodes, but rather as affordances that generate possibilities embedded in liminal, relational spaces of absence/presence that a trickster characteristically inhabits.

Is there a boundary crossing in fieldwork, one that scrambles the conventional real of 'habit memory', archaeologiness, and the unconventional unreal: the archaeologist 'haunting' the presence of the past in the present? Does the exuberance and hubris of finding "small things forgotten" in that archaeological act of discovery, foray into the shifting ground between reality and the uncanny, the archaeological etic and the ethnographic emic?

Is there just a 'trick of the trade', the creative process espoused as 'archaeologiness', tricking us with our relation to what remains of the past in the present? Is it all a 'dead end' in present time, a confusion in the archaeological encounter with 'working with' what remains of the past? Does excavation really open-up a renewal of past presence, or is this 'archaeological imagination' part of trickster personality?

Is the real story then to go beyond the contemporary storytelling directly out of the dissolution of the archaeologically (in)-habit(ed) sense of archaeologiness, outside accredited performance practices? Is it a movement toward something/someone else than a trickster? Can we associate ourselves with some real presences of the past, as ephemeral encounters with particular percolating past layers of memory? The 'trick' is to attempt this particular type of excavation!

"We go on investigating….Go on examining so much scant evidence for its least, elusive trace. Go on entering, in the ever narrowing field of a continuously expanding terminology, our own impacted data. The data, however, do not seem to bring us any closer" (Sobin 1999:44).

Are we being 'tricked' by new technologies and the comfort zone of coverage and depth they imply? There is still darkness out there. Can we in the field enter it, the 'black holes' of survey, excavation, and interpretation, and move beyond and back? Can we experience something meaningful beyond "our own sensorial 'reading' of so much extinct human landscape" (Ibid: 43)?

One way, as an example (though dealing with the ethnographic present, not the ethnographic past), is to imbricate two diachronic forms: indigenous oral narratives and archaeology (cf. Gauvreau and McLaren 2016). This approach adds "chronology, spatial information, and physical evidence of historical events" to indigenous oral narratives, as "a means of understanding the results of certain archaeological investigation from a more emic perspective" (Ibid: 304).

The material culture that we unearth, so removed from its sociocultural context that it reaches us without continuing gesture and ritual, can we still sense – experience – those traces? Is that part of the archaeological trade or do we trade it for conformity to what is expected of us as archaeologists in the academic world? Have we arrived on the scene too late to understand the performances? What if….?

These traces and fragments, are they divested of all transmissivity and contextual sensory value? Can they be associated with more than something else beyond mere 'survives time'? These same artifacts, assemblages, ruined structures, as we gaze at them through the veil and contour of absence, can they become a real sense of memory? Is this memory any different than its antecedent in the past? Is "here what's eternally there?" (Sobin 1999:133).

~John G. Sabol~

The Archaeologist as 'Ghostly' Presence:

The Spectral Politics of 'Archaeologiness'

The things that archaeologists do in the field, their performance practices, bear the memories of their own re-occupation of a site. If "those who frequent a place become part of one another's ambiance of that place" (Bierwert 1999:44), do season after season of archaeological exploration of one particular site/landscape, with their expanding etic approaches and technological advances, create a haunting ambiance in relation to other enduring past occupations?

If the present is also the past mixed together, who haunts who? Archaeologists must remember who (what occupations) came before them, and the limits of their archaeological vision. This means that we must re-evaluate our social relations to, and emic meaning of, dirt, stone, artifact, and bone.

The meaning of 'excavating' practices sometimes is grossly misplaced for the archaeological record in which they occur. If an archaeological record is not always now a dead, neutral backdrop, it becomes a setting in which "meanings are created, reproduced, transformed" (Tilley 1994:25). We

~John G. Sabol~

must be wary (and perhaps weary) of how we do fieldwork there. The question is: has 'archaeologiness' become a form of habit memory that buries, ever deeper, certain presences of the past?

Deeper still, if the archaeological site is the 'host', are people, things, and processes that are brought to the site potentially 'ghostly presences'? If archaeological behavior, measurement, field processing, and technology not only not form part of the memory and experience of a site's biographical past, do they also become representations of a haunting that 'ghost' the archaeological record (or that part of the past becoming present)? Is the intervention of excavation, the 'usual suspect' of this present haunting?

Quetzal Castaneda, for example, has argued, in his analysis of archaeological intervention at Chichen Itza in Mexico, that the ruins have been selectively reorganized by archaeologists "according to their own imaginings of the past". The result is that they are "the copy of an original that never existed", by 'standing' "in the unique place of the latter's debris" (1996:48-49). The result is that this 'ruin' reconstructed is a 'ghost' of the Mayan landscape that is present and representative:

"As long as man is affected by the image of a thing, he will regard the thing as present even though it may not exist" (Baruch Spinoza, *Ethics).*

Archaeologists, like anthropologists, become the 'ghost', a liminal position, as the go-between who (and what)

~John G. Sabol~

41

determines the movement between one culture and another. Archaeology, like anthropology, straddles "the margins of borders and boundaries the way ghosts are portrayed in the literature are doing" (Grady 2011:286). But unlike anthropologists, archaeologists do not mediate cultural exchange, or "participate in the social negotiations of meaning" (Ibid: 287). Can they? Should they?

By making what remains of a present past become a presence of contemporary memory and experience, has archaeology lost its ability to unearth other sensuous aspects of the past? By assembling what physically and visually remains, are we re-assembling a different past? Has the process of excavation and reconstruction, especially as heritage tourism, become part of what Gonzalez-Ruibal (2008) calls "the archaeology of the super-destruction of life and matter" (2008:262) that is the past present? As Christopher Woodward has said: "Ruins do not speak-We speak for them" (2001:203). But are we 'speaking' about the real past?

Has archaeology become, with its advances in technology devoid of 'emic' dimensions, a constellation of practices that 'gather' at ruins? Does this gathering involve the 'rabble' of forces that destroy it? Excavation is a destructive process, but so is reconstruction. Is a 'haunting' created, marked by the sense that what has been made is no longer important as the archaeological record? Will this process of destruction still haunt, generations of archaeologists later, as a social affordance of failed fieldwork? Are our reconstructions creating something new: broken material assemblages with a renewed power of 'haunting' ruination?

Instead of learning today what it is to be (become) an archaeologist (truly an etic perspective), let's first begin with the old resonant quality of occupying a landscape as if it still is an emic occupation: excavate performatively then and there, not 'incavate' our meaning and interpretation (at the edge of a trowel) in the here and now. Let's alter the sequence and rhythm of fieldwork to one of ethnographic participant-observation aimed toward potential attached presences. Could this be a new archaeological 'rite of passage', one that will not haunt us in the future?

Archaeology is a practice of meaning. It means different things, but also, more importantly, it should include sensing what (else) remains of an emerging past in the here and now, some of which passes through as ephemeral moments of presence. I know, however, that not all alternative ways of doing archaeology are equally valid, are consistent with the record, or carry the same scientific weight.

If "knowledge" and "interest" are always interrelated (Habermas 1968), then lack of certain knowledge can be related to a lack of interest. The baseline for questioning field practices must begin with why disinterest is prevalent. Is it because alternative means popularly produced unacceptable knowledge? The questioning then proceeds to 'unacceptable' to whom? If it is the contemporary archaeological community, then this is an etic viewpoint, not an emic one that haunts fieldwork. It also means that we do not justify intent through uninteresting narratives that contain "dense chapters of theoretical positioning and regurgitation of continental philosophers" (Bailey 2017:247). That truly is a contemporary 'ghost story'.

A Shrine to Absence

If "one of the greatest attractions of archaeology has been its ability to dig up 'real' life and livelihoods, to uncover actual behavior, even to give voice to people..." (Hudson 2014:83), why hasn't this 'attraction' transformed into the acknowledgement of continuing (still active) past agency? Is archaeological fieldwork characterized by the separation between an active contemporary social world at the dig site, and a passive dead, and lifeless material and structural residue? Where are the archaeologies of past forms of life? We don't unearth it by merely digging-up dead matter.

What really matters, one that changes absence to presence, are forms of socially-affording acts that may stimulate interaction, and forms of life as materializing sensory elements becoming present. Thus, the archaeological record is a hybrid network that still includes people, things, and those other presences of the past. This changes agency in archaeological fieldwork from one principally assigned to the activities of contemporary humans to one involving a still active past and present network of other 'things' and 'beings'.

Fieldwork becomes a series of performance practices that are forms of social affordances. If percolating network assemblages exist, they represent an agency that can form and retain fields of memory, already attached to particular landscapes as interactive 'structured deposits' of past presence. This possibility transforms field methodology that treats the archaeological record as material residues of static (embedded) material culture.

The existence of material and sensory components, both past and present in the record can allow us to identify non-extinct, distinctive social agency and situations that continue today. Do these form "vibrant matter" (Bennett 2010), representing a 'ghost culture' on the surface of ruin and/or visible absence?

This 'ghost culture', I propose, represents an assemblage of diverse, but relational, elements (things, 'bodies', affects, senses, memories) of "commingling and the contingent co-presence of diverse temporal moments" (Hamilakis 2016:173), and "temporal modalities: geological times, archaeological/historical times, human experiential times, non-human experiential times" (Ibid: 173). This creates an assemblage of temporality in 'immiscible time', that 'haunts' archaeological fieldwork. Such a mess, without context-specific performative intervention, remains in a state of liminality regarding meaning and interpretation.

That is why we need to 'excavate' into its particular layers of human/non-human 'memory', and distinguish between socio-cultural phenomena, non-human phenomena, and taphonomic processes (cf. Schiffer 1976). This opens up the field of fieldwork because "the wider the range of temporal (and social) possibilities, the more open will be the field of emerging situations, events, new arrangements" (Hamilakis 2016:175). This would help eliminate excavation as a shrine to particular absences (the becoming of past memories of experience), helping to eliminate the 'black holes' that are found in many archaeological narratives and site reports:

"We engage with a fragment of the actual existing reality of human existences, not a record of their absence" (Barrett 2016:135).

Do absent presences have continuing "presence effects" (Gumbrecht 2004) that go beyond visual, reconstructed, and imaginative archaeological records? Does this presence, despite archaeological intervention, "interrupt, perturb, and haunt fixed persons, places, or things" (Anderson 2009:18)? Do they manifest in the form of "leaks...and ruptures as they transgress normative territories of feeling" (Arojona 2015:4)? Do archaeological sites 'host' these 'structures of feeling'? Is absent presence, especially reports of personal experiences, in archaeological field reports, part of this absent reality? Does contemporary excavations, as an 'etic' penetration, perturb them?

Do these 'structures of feeling' form another baseline for the acquisition of knowledge that suggests traces of a present (not absent) presence? Is this particular presence part of what John C. Barrett (2016) acknowledges as absent presence?

"What will it take for archaeology to operate not as if its role were to interpret the representations of the past but to engage with that part of the reality of the past that exists today"? (Barrett 2016:135)

~John G. Sabol~

Such a possibility requires us to develop relational assemblages of practices (as "presence effects") that can afford emergences of past sensualities to occur today. This means isolating and unearthing a past memory of experience (as a 'form of life') through particular 'excavating' performance practices.

~John G. Sabol~

The 'Black Holes' of Archaeological Excavation

Are we defining archaeology in terms of 'etic' distance, rather than a communicating discipline that really works with what remains of the past? Does excavation create 'black holes' rather than unearthing a more sensual presence of the past? Are these 'black holes' inhabited (characterized) by "memory, ghosts, moonlight, and weeds" (Chard 1999)? Is this vision more than a romantic, imaginative view of ruins (a 'ruin porn') or the contemporary presence of the past?

Are these 'black holes' the result of an insensitivity to a sensorial experience of the past (and not its present excavation)? Beyond the buckets of earth removed, the dimensions of spaces and objects located and measured, a surface plowed and an area scanned, is this all that exists of the past? Michael Shanks (1991) has said this:

"Archaeology excavates a hollow. There is an emptiness. The raw existence of the past is not enough, insufficient in itself...what is needed is our desire to fill the hollow, raise the dead. This is archaeology's necromancy" (1991:114).

We don't re-occupy a site during excavation. We cover-up much sensually by sometimes creating a past senseless hole. We further darken these holes through academic or political 'etics', rather than re-enlighten them through social 'emics'. Finding our way around in the past should not end at twilight or at the trowel's edge. That it does means that we rely too much on vision, rather than a visionary, sensorial approach, sympathetic to experiencing the past, that archaeology should foster. This approach must become context-specific to those ephemeral, ethnographic moments that materialize during the excavation process.

The 'archaeologiness – that rite of archaeological passage – is a very different sensual experience than that experienced by past audiences and occupations. How do we fill-in these 'dark holes', within our attempts at interpretation? If archaeology is the study of memory (Olivier 2008), then it must remember the spaces of darkness that remain un(or under)-performed in excavating a site, as we work with what remains.

When do remains become archaeologically-framed? Being buried under the earth, a vertical descent, and being exposed through excavation as material culture, is one criteria of framing the past. But sometimes those spaces and experiences perceived as being 'dead to the world' and forgotten are too often neglected or ignored. Do they still contain 'vibrant matter'?

Let's shift the 'how' of fieldwork, and the position of the archaeologist, as defined by/from time (the present) and space (a ruin/absent presence) to what we can do that defines some episode or exposure as sensually archaeological. This would position contemporary archaeological fieldwork into a social dialogue between

~John G. Sabol~

archaeologists, past presence, place, subjective experience, and a 'performance' excavation. This entangled relationship can become an archaeological 'witnessing' of past sensual continuity between present and past.

Though archaeological interventions are sensual fieldwork, employing aspects (besides sight) of touch and smell on site, and taste in experiments, these are not sensually context-specific to what may remain active. They become present in contemporary (etic) sensual fields. There is no transduction (passing from one medium to another) of space, time, and experience. A past sensorium does not become breached. Fieldwork remains translation, not a past memory field.

Archaeology has habitually focused (as a 'habit memory') on what surface and subsurface material traces remain. Little, if any, attention is directed toward ongoing ephemeral trans-spatial/temporal sensual movements between past and present. Such presences remain in the dark as these 'black holes' of fieldwork. They create, if unexplored, an affordance than can evolve into an archaeological 'ghostscape'.

~John G. Sabol~

The 'Haunting' of a Site

An archaeological excavation, with its etic-bounded 'archaeologiness' in excavation practice, enforces purposes and meaning, once buried in layers of memory, to be scraped away and replaced by newer archaeological ones. An excavation does not react successfully with, to use Ingolds' term, the "temporality of the landscape". It does not perform to, but rather haunts, a landscape's role as a store of memory (Bender 2002) and experience.

How might excavation performances call to mind, for example, Keith Basso's account of how locations within the landscape are the bearers of moral values for the Western Apache (Basso 1984)? How does this affect the archaeological record? Does archaeological excavation, instead of unearthing the sensibility and sensitivity of the past and its presences, become a "landscape of provocation" (Massey 2006) to certain memories of the past?

Does archaeology 'stage' its relationship with the past, creating a 'front door' for reconstructive experience, as its 'back door' memory is largely ignored? If a site's full potential (that part archaeologists are 'working with') is based on cultural resonance, not only physical recognition of strata and associations, how is digging remembering that resonance? If resonance is the power to evoke memory in the present of a past presence, how 'powerfully' effective is the excavation process?

An archaeological excavation is a 'haunting'. It 'haunts' specific spaces by creating a particular 'etic' rhythm, a ritual of 'habit memory' that embeds a contemporary presence that is disassociated from past rhythms of how things happened in certain spaces. This is not just the idea that the medium ('etic' performance as excavation) is a spectral messaging to what remains 'active' of the past in the present, it also incorporates a different ('other') category of social being. This social being, the archaeologist, emerges in the everyday repeated performance of excavation.

Excavation takes us to the 'etics' of contemporary site formation processes which lies at the heart of an archaeological 'ethics' toward the presence of past forms of life. Even the 'script' of archaeological behavior and dialogue need evaluation. Its 'etic', not 'emically' related to the layers of memory in the archaeological record, is the contemporary rite of passage that transforms a 'digger' into an 'archaeologist'.

What remains after the 'event' of excavation (beyond material culture) is our archaeological question. At the core of this archaeological question is trauma, what was lost, transformed, suppressed, forgotten, and newly-inscribed. This trauma is a widening gap, between what remained before excavation began, and what accretions are now attached to the excavated spaces.

~John G. Sabol~

Michael Shanks once suggested (2002, at the SAA meeting in Denver): "ask us to look to our own practices" to determine if archaeology is "really about knowing the past". Instead of aiming for an exposure of, or closure to, the past, let's open it up! Let's begin to conceive of some past elements as sometimes existing as real-time events. This is not a mobilization of the past so that it can play an active role in the present, so much as it is, first and foremost, to document those potential real-time events.

If the archaeological record is composed of these residues of events (cf. Shennan 1993), does contemporary excavations create social affordances that are still capable of affording the past becoming present? Can non-resonant excavations that uncover (not recover) past 'dead' situations become a process that can transform a perceived static archaeological record to a dynamic one? Can these 'events' be sensory artifacts or assemblages that persist for a greater duration than an uncovered (buried) material context?

The archaeological gaze during excavation, despite a recent focus on the sensualness of doing fieldwork, has still produced a limited experience of what remains of the past besides material culture. It is a 'pre-cissing' of what archaeological excavation can produce sensually from the record of past occupations.

A concern with the "discipline of the space" (Olsen et.al. 2012:61)focuses on a hidden archaeological record, a physical and ontological disconnect from the present that requires an 'unearthing' through excavation. This creates a temporal barrier: without excavation, there is no past in the present. Hence, 'archaeologiness', defining an archaeological profile, requires some form of digging, despite recent endeavors in an "archaeology of the contemporary world" (Graves-Brown et.al. 2013).

Is archaeology too much a gravitational pull to unearth and expose the earth without attempting much effort to sense other potential sensorial presences?

"Shattered, ruined places and objects assume a material presence that presents us with a seemingly formless, ungrounded chaos" (Adam Lovase).

Does this produce contemporary, mythic archaeological field reports and narratives that present a past 'ghostscape'?

If some of the archaeological record is not grounded, then archaeology must loosen its seemingly sacred ground of 'archaeologiness' attached to survey and excavation. That chaos, as that ungrounded mess, becomes a continuing sensitivity of past spaces, amid hidden layers of attached memory on the surface of ruin, abandonment, and absent presence. Appearances do not necessarily equate to the absence of presence. We make it so.

These produce 'stratigraphic inversions', not of physical ground or material culture, but embedded and attached memories "below the thresholds at which visibility begins" (DeCerteau 1984:93). Their manifestations constitute a type of 'noise' within the usual tropes of survey and excavation. Are these embedded/attached 'noises' assemblages of local knowledge within past 'mindscapes'? Are they built around academic or political "structures of forgetting" (Hamilton 1994:13) that create affordances of loss?

Are archaeological excavations assembling a past that is, in some aspects of sensitivity, "matter out of place" (Douglas 1966:36)? Is the past really 'out' of places and spaces? How can we investigate "assemblages of humans and non-humans which are the product of a series of historical processes by which they are jumbled together in the present (Harrison 2011:157)?

The specialty of archaeology is the "abandoned place" but not all fieldwork is conducted within spaces of dead and abandoned presence. Is archaeology merely a clearance and reassembly of particular traces of the past in the present? Are some places more 'memoryscapes' of presence, rather than spaces for clearance? Are some areas still a "practiced place" (deCerteau 1984:117), where sensory elements still percolate on the surface of ruin? By clearing the space, without affording something to emerge, are we allowing that space to remain dead, changing these 'memoryscapes' to a 'ghostscape'?

Should archaeologists call for a "sociology of things that aren't there", an "agnotology" or "absentology" (Croissant 2014:18)? Could (should) this include, beside material culture (as "vibrant matter') percolating, ephemeral sensory elements?

Are we missing informants, not as indigenous peoples, but the archaeologists themselves? If some 'scapes' still materialize and become present during fieldwork, why do we oft times negate such 'witnessing'? If history is a dead subject, and the material objects unearthed by archaeologists, the 'ghosts' of the past, what is it that still haunts the contemporary archaeological record? What else returns and becomes a contemporary presence? What haunts us more in the field: past memories of 'archaeologiness' or these contemporary 'ghosts'?

~John G. Sabol~

<u>Why?</u>

A Disrupted Archaeological Record as the Present

"If the historical past be knowable, it must belong to the present world of experience".

- Michael Oakeshott (1933:107)

What is 'proper' archaeology, and what is not?

"The goal of archaeology is to open people's minds and disrupt received perceptions of society, politics, places, peoples, and material culture" (Bailey 2017:695).

Such an archaeology must become 'excavating' performance practices that go beyond the 'usual suspects' of 'archaeologiness', what Pierce (1998) calls habit. This is the "repetition and patterning of socially construed meaning" (Bauer 2013:16). Those 'habit memories' of excavation, beyond the continuum of past to present description and classification of people and material culture, are not simple (or simply) stories of the past. This is because continuing presences still manifest as echoes of disarticulated, lingering social issues.

These presences disrupt traditional archaeological contexts, disordering existing knowledge in a form of 'deviant' archaeology. It is an affecting appearance that begs intervention, one usually ignored or dismissed. This disruption is both an outcome of residual (environmental) processes at work and, in some cases, a social act with intention. It identifies a path to presence that is usually unacknowledged during excavation.

These manifestations must be acknowledged for what they are: that the past only ever exists in that moment of becoming present through technological scans, surface surveys, excavation, and percolating materializations. There is more to place and space, room to make these connections archaeologically beyond the scans articulated grid and the scope of laboratory analysis. Let's re-purpose the narrow assumption that there is only one truth to be told, that there is one standard process of assembling/re-assembling what remains.

Let's end 'gate-keeping' contexts of 'stillborn' pasts awaiting extraction and removal, and open wide that door to a past still becoming present. Let's re-look the idea of what it still means to be in that (not this) world, a world that still has not past but remains present.

Excavation as intent is a concern with a particular fieldwork disposition that oft times hides time, sensory elements, and active agency. We must transform our traditional rite of passage into the past so that we may experience the archaeological record in a different way, perhaps in a way that our perceptions of it acquires a resonance to those memories that are dislocated from what archaeologists have come to expect (or speculate/imagine).

~John G. Sabol~

The result of this re-orientation to fieldwork and excavation habits is a triggering mechanism for more sensual experiences within archaeological practices. Let's continue to break free, beyond the trowel's edge, digging deeper into the record than what we had previously imagined. Let's loosen the constraints of standard academic practices.

Part of this exploratory exercise, however, does not lie in entering forms of popular cultural practices, such as those of 'ghost hunting' (cf. Beashaw 2016)? It remains, within the remains of sensually unearthing traces of a past sensorium within a specific layer of memory. It involves bringing one's own particular experience and skill sets to focus on common archaeological problems.

In my particular situation, this includes 'method acting' and developing context-specific cultural scenarios for immersive simulations. This is a relational tradition in archaeological fieldwork of more than surface genealogical roots (cf. Tilley 1989; Pearson and Shanks 2001, among others). This is not just another way of interpreting the past. It becomes a 'reoccupation' (not a representation or re-construction) of the past.

This immersion questions, even before the contemporary archaeological occupation has ended, the complex issues of absence and presence in a site or landscape of overt, visual past emptiness. It further asks the question: what effect (or social affordance) has archaeological excavation and on-site contemporary performance practices created after the excavated remains have been exposed and/or removed from sense and site.

How does what archaeology did there (the words, movements, acts, emotions, intentions, and thoughts) have on an excavated site? Have the 'etics' of archaeological intervention and politics changed forever the locations' 'emic' archaeological record? Does this then become a question of archaeological ethics? What becomes of memory in the archaeological record? What becomes the memory of life before the archaeological interruptions?

~John G. Sabol~

<u>The Vertical Imaginary:</u>

<u>Excavations into Sense(filled)</u>
<u>Surfaces</u>

Is there a relationship to vertical space in archaeology other than excavation? Are there assemblages of remains, as sensory elements, that connect the plane of excavation (the surface) to a radically different sense of the past? Is this one that vertically percolates upward toward contemporary reality? Is this related to some embedded and/or attached memories of occupation that have not been forgotten, and not 'built' upon by succeeding re-occupations? Do ephemeral traces "enable movement by bringing two spaces in relation" (Bridge 2013:55)? Does it create a vertical imaginary as horizontal reality?

This imaginary becoming present opens excavation to intertwined spaces of vertical/horizontal cultural entanglement: an enmeshed, knotted meeting of the 'etic' excavator with a potential 'emic' presence of the past? Can such encounters, if they occur, be (or become) sociable? Are they inseparable from archaeological intervention, or merely an alternative archaeological imagination, one seldom explored?

Such potential conduits of contact can connect places, remains, temporalities, and meaning. They can become

~John G. Sabol~

vehicles of powerful social narratives that still haunt, not merely 'ghost stories'. They circulate tension, commitment, change, struggle and other affordances that may remain important processes of both stability and transformation that are presences that can still be experienced. They are other stories to be archaeologically uncovered.

Can archaeology become the intermediary in this 'vertical turn' to fieldwork? Can it assume a secondary, liminal position between an emerging (emic) past and a descending contemporary immersive (etic) excavation? Going beyond the archaeological imagination, can they become a collection of time-space elements in need of chronicling (as a presence sense of reality)? Can they become important spaces of connectivity between the surface, still unexcavated sub-surface, archaeological practice, situated performance, mess, and a still 'vibrant' ground? Does it co-mingle past and present, emic and etic elements?

This imaginary cum reality moves us away from excavation as vertical 'depth' to presences as percolating verticality. It alters our sense of and sensitivity toward spaces archaeologically. It alters surface composition. It negates linearity. It expands philosopher Peter Sloterdijks' suggestion (1999) of spherical constellations of meaning that envisage urban space as an enclosed sphere stretched by shared habitation to include landscapes of/in ruin. This arising and arresting verticality suggests interconnecting spaces of function and meaning populated with the memories of people often invisible in the historical record.

~John G. Sabol~

We must re-visit the logistics of excavation, its physical processes, its neglected performative function, its potentially destructive social element. We must re-work that etic relationship to include emic parameters, the affecting role of new technologies on old memories, and their relation to fields of potentially embedded and attached presence in our perceptions of space.

This re-working of archaeological 'digging' becomes, not 'reverse archaeology' as 'incavation' (an intervening presence of the present into the layers of the past), but a reverse stratigraphy of presence, a thrust from the past not a dig into it. Archaeology can provide a greater awareness of the interconnectivities between time, space, and memory as the worlds that we inhabit, and those that we excavate, collapse into the reality of actuality: a time that is neither past nor present, but rather a future configuration becoming present.

~John G. Sabol~

Sense and Sensitivity: The 'Other' Ethnographic Perspective

As we excavate and immerse ourselves into artifacts and features of the past, is the encounter more than a representative sample of the presence of the past? What else might transpire within the interaction between people and things? What transformation (or transduction) might occur between these archaeological things and the perceiving human body?

Are there other realities, embedded and attached, of relationality and presence other than those perceived archaeologically by the living, by the human? Is it a question of perspective: instead of the present viewing an emerging past through excavation, is it perhaps also an emerging present being perceived by a past presence, humans becoming present in the past archaeological record? 'Who' is sensing 'what'?

This perspective is a sense of relational perspectivism, one grounded in lived and still 'living' experience, as a tool of excavation. This archaeologically 'excavating' perspectivism by sensing humans (archaeologists), as actors and 'makers', sensibly co-create the world of the past becoming present with other entities, rather than standing back etically to think and observe from a temporal distance. Is this the 'other' side ethnographically of a grounded emic perspective?

Such an archaeological perspectivism, I propose, involves the vital materiality of things (cf. Santos-Granero 2009), and the vibrancy of past space. It includes the persistence of presence and social memory. It is about how encounters (both residually incidental and socially-directed) during fieldwork can create transformations in our usual perception of the archaeological record.

If "all archaeology is about memory" (Hamilakis 2010:188), and if memory serves as a link between past and present, then memory becomes a form of 'relatedness', eradicating boundaries by the practice of sameness with particular worlds and other beings (cf. Bird-David 1999). Memory, and its recall, creates meaningful relationships.

Meaning is inherent in the "relational context of people's direct perceptual engagement (i.e. the archaeologists) with the world...derived from a practical background of involved activity" (Willerslev 2007:20). Such involving activity could occur during excavations into the past of still meaningful spaces. This engagement becomes an ethnographic experience, not an orientation (an enculturation) into the ways of a professional archaeologist (the 'archaeologiness' of fieldwork).

Digging into a Sensory Palimpsest

Archaeological excavations often dig at sites that are "spatial palimpsest" (Abbas 1994), producing "a weakening of the sense of chronology, of historical sequentiality, so that old and new are easily contemporaneous and continuities and discontinuities exist side by side" (1994:448). In such places, time is archaeological 'immiscible': it does not attain homogeneity. It moves forward, but is also subject to repetition and return. Can the same be said for a site's sensorium?

Do some sensory elements, as artifacts of past occupations, senses of place never really dead and buried, remain embedded and attached to the archaeological record? Do such percolating, immiscible sensorial temporalities alter the 'habit memory' of archaeological fieldwork (as an element of 'archaeologiness'), or are they simply ignored?

If space knows no duration, only the present (Bergson 1889 (2001)), are archaeological spaces, excavated in the present, and archaeologists (as contemporary presences) part of the archaeological record of what remains? Can sensory elements of presence, attached to certain spaces, endure, not thru time but as immiscible temporalities that remain forms of life (not mere echoes of the past, dead and buried)?

~John G. Sabol~

Archaeological fieldwork is basically an immiscible time frame. It is not 'in sync' with the rhythms of site occupation, even though unearthing what remains is done in situ. The archaeology now is not occupation now, even though the space may be shared. If archaeology is a craft, the craft of archaeology is to be <u>in</u> time and <u>of</u> time. It is to entangle with those layers present of memory, and not the 'habit memory' of archaeological fieldwork.

These residues of other times present can sometimes be socially affecting residues. They touch things and persons during fieldwork, experiences that are no longer entirely 'here', but still present:

"A repeated gesture, an aged object...a footprint...all of these things, material and immaterial might drag something of the no longer now...into the present, or drag the present into the no longer now" (Schneider 2014:45).

An archaeologist who works with this past, and within this 'in situ' context, is already a part of that immiscible time in the present (and into the future). This affect, perhaps prompted by a sensory element other than visual, is an immaterial residue that creates a visionary sensation of presence.

The ground of fieldwork changes, becoming unfamiliar to 'habit memory', the 'archaeologiness' of a dig site. It allows our senses to become alert to "the reappearance of what has been supposed to have gone forever" (Lamb 2010:17).

~John G. Sabol~

This is not now the past. It is the present, manifesting memory.

Is this memory a replay of percolating sensory elements that know no duration, what Rebecca Schneider (2014) calls theatre, a "kind of living archaeology, or archaeology of the live" (2014:60)? Are we missing this still living theatrical presence in the archaeological present?

~John G. Sabol~

<u>*Fearful Interruptions in Sociable Stratigraphy*</u>

The archaeological record is not linear. We all know that. But one interruption, manifesting two worlds/two times, sometimes surfaces and antagonistically has implications which have largely been ignored in fieldwork. This interruption too is part of excavation stories. They occur as immiscible times, forms of traces of other realities that vie for presence within ruin, rubble, and excavation space. The question is: can archaeology re-focus "upon the gap (this interruption, I propose) between the lived past and its ruin now" (Shanks 1992)?

Do such interruptions correspond to Stolers' (2013) definition of ruins as those "sites that condense alternative senses of history" (2013:9)? Does an experience of this interruption represent time as a "chronotope" (Bakhtin 1981), "representing the inseparability of space and time" (1981:85)? If so, these presences, excavated as a chronotopic layer of memory, would be an etic interruption of an emic continuity of occupation.

Perhaps the possibility of these presences (in an embedded 'sociable stratigraphy') illustrate the way things (as a 'sensory ghost') and spaces, within a particular site or landscape, can produce (or afford) spectral appearances? This spectral afterlife may also indicate the continuing

~John G. Sabol~

memory of a shift in situation at a site that once involved individuals or groups: a change in socio-political or socio-economic status, perhaps? Does it represent a longing for past conditions that still remain vibrant? Such spatial interruptions speak to primordial fears and desires.

There are landscapes that are haunted by these extended emotions, a trauma that moves forward through time. The exposed and excavated presence of objects and structures, once buried, afford these extended emotions to surface. This lingering spatial presence creates an atmosphere, a sensitivity to intrusion and intervention.

Does archaeological intervention add an embedded sense of fear, altering the scenarios of the past? Let's not further amplify and extend excavation destruction by ignoring these percolating emotions that hold memories of other past presences. In archaeological space, the archaeologist (or someone else) may still hear them scream.

~John G. Sabol~

Plurimediated Presence: The Para-Sociality of Archaeological Re-Occupation

A site's archaeological record, its ruined present, is connected to multiple pasts by a social process that continues to evolve. This record of a percolating past presence becomes a form of "para-social interaction" (Horton and Wohl 1956). Past percolations produce contemporary storylines and a relationship toward those stories. Why do we continually leave these stories out of site reports? Is it because the archaeological 'object', par excel lance, is the study and recovery of material remains (Bradley 2000)?

What does the past demands of us, those whose principal concern is to unearth it? It demands, I propose, an idea of presence adequate to its ontological record, not only what its material culture shows. These multiple interactions within the archaeological record defy academic and archaeological politics. These politics are 'etic' concerns, not the possible continuing sociality of the presence of the past.

In excavation, changing our perspectives only becomes sensed over time and through the exposure of material

~John G. Sabol~

culture within layers of memory deposition. Archaeological performance as social interaction with this presence, rather than an excavation solely of material remains, creates a space of learning, the sensual transformation of reality into socio-cultural imaginaries.

These "social imaginaries" create cultural experiences at a site in which a multiplicity of experiences, practices, and relationships are mediated (cf. Shepherd 2007). Let's re-occupy those imaginaries during our brief, but potentially socially destructive, archaeological intervention at our sites of fieldwork.

~John G. Sabol~

The Excavation of Past Futures:

The 'Host', the 'Ghost', and Archaeological Intervention

Has archaeology become merely the "discipline of things" (Witmore 2014:203)? Do these things, as the contemporary version of the archaeological record, get on 'just fine' without the benefit of human intervention and interpretation (Ibid: 217)? Are there no consequences to how we excavate the past? Is the challenge merely to produce rich descriptive accounts of things? Is this so-called "return to things" lacking the dynamics, the social affordances that allow archaeologists to work with the presences of the past?

Does archaeological intervention close, by enclosing itself in mere things, a future past for other forms of presence to emerge? Does the 'host', the site of intervention, experience a 'ghostly presence' in the form of archaeological excavation? Are archaeologists, like archaeological sites, persons and places of haunting, the return to something in uncanny form? Does this create, through excavation, an interruption for those forms of life

~John G. Sabol~

still present as the archaeological record? Does excavation become a 'staging ground', the future tense of social destruction?

"We are ourselves producers of archaeological materials...we do little more than add a new archaeological episode to the existence of places and things that have already known a long series of functions and uses" (Olivier 2001:180).

This "new archaeological episode", however, can evolve the archaeological site into spaces that are not a place of their time(s), regarding some occupational presences of the past. If the "ghost is not simply a dead or missing person, but a social figure" (Gordon 1997:8), is that 'ghost' the archaeologist? Is it because archaeological intervention is merely another layer of memory practices that haunts?

Is excavation, then, a form of "destructive production" (Gordillo 2014:81)? Does it lay "waste to certain people, relations, and things" (Stoler 2013:11), creating ghostly presences amid percolating past layers of memory becoming present?

Between the survey and the excavation, there occurs a liminal space, "experiential space" (Couclelis 1992):

"Experiential space...is the space human beings actually experience before it is passed through the filters of scientific analysis" (Ibid: 229).

Have you experienced it in the field? No? Is it because, beside a fear of academic folly, such acknowledgement creates stories that are subversive, reminding us how politically and etically constructed the archaeological record can be (really is)? Such experiences render opaque the social processes which afford and normalize our traditional archaeological sense, our everyday 'habit memory' of fieldwork. Yet these experiences permit a tolerable trace of the 'emic' indigenous: not the contemporary ethnographic one, but rather those context-specific to past occupations.

Karen Holmberg (2013) has said this:

"While acknowledging the archaeological limitations on what we can plausibly say about the bodily experience of the past, I hold...that the senses form an important ghost of adventure to explore..." (2013:63).

Let's make that archaeological 'ghost' a sensible, sensitive, and contextually-relational being. Let's not haunt the future. Those archaeological interventions into past and present occupations need not be socially destructive, ones that sometimes bury (not unearth) the presence of fieldwork actuality. Let's entertain these occasional, ephemeral moments of discovery, and work with them.

~John G. Sabol~

<u>Memory: Inscriptions and Erasures</u>

"Memory is not an instrument for exploring the past, but rather a medium. It is the medium of that which is experienced, just as earth is the medium in which ancient cities lie buried".

- Walter Benjamin (1932:576)

The archaeological record, its 'archaeologiness', both in terms of discipline and documentation emerges from particular provenances: digging it up, surveying its surface parameters, or uncovering through technological means what lies underneath ground and environmental obstacles. Data and its interpretation are based on both behavioral and transformational processes as human and natural interventions (cf. Ashmore and Sharer 2000:60-67).

But what about a different form of deposition, one that holds the past rather than is the past itself, a memory rather than material culture in situ? If the medium is memory within a stratigraphic-like surface record, rather than physically being excavated, what do we do then? What if this memory includes not only the past in the present, but also the present in the past as a form of social affordance?

What if both are sensed, performed, and produced as an "archaeology of trauma, emotion, and intimate involvement" (Gonzalez-Rubio 2008:248). What if this is an archaeology of 'them' (past occupations) not us, who, then are those alive, and who are the dead, the 'ghosts'?

The transformation of the archaeological record into important statements of (and about) memory are achieved through their juxtaposition and entanglement to distinctive performance practices and contexts (cf. Barrett 1988:31-2). This achievement can occur if archaeologists attempt to afford opportunities for past practices to be remembered and executed in the field. This forms a new rite of passage in archaeological intervention. It becomes a 'ritual time' that can transform certain aspects of the past, as different fields of memory emerge and become present.

A 'Ritual' Time of Present Passage

Does archaeology need, as Gonzales-Ruibal (2016) recently argued, a more complex conceptualization of time? Is there a time of contemporary presence which differs from the memory of archaeological excavation? How are layers of memory within pasts given a time of presence in the present etic practices of archaeological fieldwork? Do we need a particular "timework" (Flaherty 2011), a way of documenting different operational forms of time, as part of materializing forms of life?

Time, in this context, is not a locator/relational tool. It is something active sensually. This recasts time as something to be sensed as ongoing phenomena: some 'times' are still lived, enacted, and performed. Is this a time "to make room for ghosts" (Gonzales-Ruibal 2016:159)? Does "making room" produce certain experiences of the past that are temporally ephemeral?

Is this particular duration part of the excavation process, or does it require other practices in 'excavating'? Can we use the concept of "timework", not as duration or finality, (i.e. a completely static archaeological record at 'time' of excavation), but as transformation, one that changes the archaeological record to an emerging social and performative time of emerging presences? Is this what

Fowles (2013) calls "doings", a particular field practice that can work with these ephemeral remains of the past?

Fieldwork becomes the enactment of a rite of passage, not as a transformation to a professional archaeologist, but as a re-occupation of place within a particular layer of memory:

- <u>Separation</u>: at the site of the dig, we leave the present for the past: performance practices that 'target' a particular layer of memory;
- <u>Liminality:</u> it begins by sensing what affect (if any) participation in past spaces and practices affords and materializes a different experience of 'archaeologiness'; and
- <u>Reincorporation</u>: Performance reiterations to what materializes sensually from that layer of memory as a re-occupation of site.

This rite of passage implies that the archaeological record, at least in part, can be defined by enfolding the distance (as 'archaeological time') between past production and contemporary re-production, rather than excavation destruction. Rather than merely investigating a site as an exclusive past of what visibly remains, might it not be more productive to work with what may materialize during attempts at re-occupation, and how traces of past occupations may be experienced today as still 'vibrant', sensual matter?

~John G. Sabol~

Expanding sites made meaningful by contemporary human intervention, rather than excavation 'recovery', frees fieldwork from the ruin and the monumental (cf. deNardi 2012:281). This is a way of engaging archaeologists in "meaningful places" (Bowser and Zedeno 2009). Could this rite of passage, creating contemporary 'emic' (not 'etic') meaningful places be a form of "persistent place" (Schlanger 1992), abandoned archaeological sites where, for example, percolating sensory manifestations show evidence of continuing use?

Do memories that won't go away, embedded in these places, become attached to particular persons, situations and objects? Does it create a sense of place that is more than the 'ghosts of place'? The what (and 'who') archaeologists engage with immerses with, rather than distancing from, subjective experiences of fields of embedded/attached memories.

It can lead to fieldwork as a form of social technology, a knowledge about how one does something (cf. Hacking 1996). That something is a performance excavation, transformed from a physical extraction to context-specific acts. Can we apply a social life to archaeological fieldwork in, not beyond, the trenches or at night? Can we define this social life as a form of ritualization? Bell (1997) has defined ritualization as "the simple imperative to do something in such a way that the doing itself gives the act a special or privileged status" (1997:168). Does it create a contemporary, 'emic' meaningful place?

~John G. Sabol~

Is this doing something meaningful a "doings" (Fowles 2013)? Is ritualization, in this form, "timework": where we make time in a particular way? Laidlaw (1994) argues that ritualization is a particular series of framing actions, and it is this framing as a "ritual attitude" that is critical. It becomes a social technology of time management that allows us to unfold past and present by 'doing' particular 'timework'-related immersive practices, ones that resonate with specific past occupational memories.

This becomes 'social life' whereby the archaeologist becomes an agent that transforms the archaeological record from 'dead' to "vibrant matter" (Bennett 2010). Do these "timework"-related immersive practices bring about this transformation of "the causal milieu in such a way as can only be attributed to their (the archaeologist's) agency" (Gell 1998:20)?

This "timework", as a social tool of excavation, creates a ritual time that renews the 'time' that binds certain presences to a particular space, experience, situation, and memory. It extends presence past the present and into the future. It is a form of "ghost ethnography" (Ferrell 2015; 2016). This involves the ability to "excavate absence" in order to sense and experience "who is not there" (unseen in the scene of physical 'digging').

Archaeological work must move from professional "time detectives" (Fagan 1995) to presenting archaeologists as 'time-benders', through contemporary ritualistic rhythms, and entangling social affordances (as 'social technologies')

~John G. Sabol~

83

relative to context-specific memories. This is contemporary archaeology's "timework" in working with what traces of a sensorium of past occupations still remain in the archaeological record.

~John G. Sabol~

How: The Reset

<u>*Profiling at the Scene of Materialization*</u>

Our practices in the excavation process, as a physical assemblage of tasks, many times narrows its potentiality as a research tool. As Timothy Darvill (2015) observes:

"Excavation is not just a technical process; it is an opportunity to use the physical and intellectual space created by the work itself to develop and refine credible understandings of the past at the point of dissection" (2015:107).

Are uncanny percolations of presence an indicator (or social affordance) of an incomplete act, situation, or ritual? Can we, how do we, dissect an incomplete past process, a rite of passage, or even a simple mundane act terminated before completion? Most excavations have suffered from 'body-shaped holes' of absent presence (except of course in the context of a burial). The presence of humans is implied but their embedded memories are still largely out of reach as an interpretation at the trowel's edge.

Archaeological excavation creates a certain rhythmic profile and path to the past. Most times this rhythm does not coincide with the profiles of memory that remain embedded in the archaeological record. This is an important absent profile recovery. Henri Lefebvre (2004) has said this:

"Everywhere where there is interaction between a place, a time, and an expenditure of energy, there is rhythm" (2004:15).

Archaeological excavations are more focused on the rhythmic 'etics' of a site's physical transformations than the 'emics' of continuity of social rhythms of a site's past occupational profiles. How does this rhythmic change transform the profiles of memory of the past?

If the archaeological record is a series of spaces of polyrhythmic ensembles contained within layers of both embedded and attached presences of memory, how do we excavate sensibly the sensual nature of these assemblages? Michael Ondaatje (2000) writes: "a good archaeologist can read a bucket of soil as if it were a complex historical novel" (2000:151). But can they sense (and react) to those percolating profiles of memories?

We must target for excavation these rhythmic patterns when they manifest, not ignore them. At these times, we must perform to this appeal, the testimony of the uncanny 'eyewitness', not the spade or trowel. This 'testimony', as materializing ephemeral sensory profiles, is not a form of "ethnographic ventriloquism". It's the opening of an 'ontological moment' in a layer of space/time memory: between a past closure and the present disclosure.

~John G. Sabol~

This 'ethnographic moment' differs from those objects found and already-brought-together that represent the "sum of human activities" (Renfrew and Bahn 2008:578) in the archaeological record. It is a more dynamic notion: 'profile memory assemblages'. The emergence of this 'profile memory' is based on archaeological, context-specific, rhythmic acts. This is a "deliberate act of bringing things and entities in association, of coming together, stressing the agency involved in this process" (Hamilakis and Jones 2017:80).

Deliberate acts in the form of 'profiling' helps to diminish the archaeologist as 'trickster' by not affording certain contemporary expectations (the 'etic' of 'archaeologiness'), and conforming behaviors in the name of science. This 'unearths' an assemblage of experiences, those normally outside one's scope of cultural perception and production as an archaeologist. The 'trickster' perception of archaeologists is not new. In 1948, W.W. Taylor criticized his colleagues for their limited 'archaeologiness': "productivity is doing whatever other archaeologists do…".

This 'profiling' of memory becomes an experience of exploration. We cannot be habitually confined (a la "Time Team" programming) to any one or two modes of sensory search input, or the intensification of more precise and sophisticated visual aids. We must become involved within a broader context-specific sensory register.

Any 'interpretation at the trowel's edge', or a remote sensor's gaze, begins primarily as a 'ghost' occupation to absent forms of past life. They do not reveal traces of past occupational presence that may still remain 'actively' present. The ruin remains, a presence still absent, and agency is still a process of transduction, from one medium (passivity) to another (activity). That there remain presences in positions of access still remains to be profiled. That they do not have the character of 'archaeologiness' is a factor in why they are not warranting or commanding attention and further exposure.

If, as Walter Benjamin (2003) asserted, that the past has not budged and piles up in front of our eyes (2003:392), much of the archaeological record (and this includes ephemeral, percolating manifestations) does not need to be physically excavated. If it gathers into potentially new (future) pasts as fields of memory (cf. Olivier 2011), some of this profile emerges through timely archaeological re-occupations. But can we perceive these 'sediments' and sentiments of memory beyond the mess of fieldwork politics?

Has 'archaeologiness' created a 'workscape' that both filters and suppresses particular past presences? Has it avoided the plausible telling of specific kinds of narratives? Does this create large segments of 'uninhabited (and unimagined) landscapes, an environment that is itself yet "pregnant with the past" (Ingold 1993:152)?

We must conceive of new time sensitive ('birthing') tools that can create an emergent "pregnancy of possibility" (Crouch 2010:1). Can we engage this "zone of transaction" in such a way that "needs to be understood in terms of what it does" (Dorrian and Rose 2003:16), instead of the imaginary of 'archaeologiness'? What happens when once immiscible archaeological work practices (when working with what remains) now become sensed 'live' and timely documented by an archive (video and/or audio recordings)?

"It's a question of 'time': to suggest that time may be touched, crossed, visited, or revisited, that time is transitive and flexible, that time may recur in time, that time is not one – never only one..." (Schneider 2011:30).

The way we live 'in time' in the field can give rise to new values of archaeological concern. The sense of behavior and production, entangled during profiling, can become human social presence and agency.

The intent to pursue this becomes an alternative to materiality, the rejection of linear temporalities, the ruin as non-ruin, and abandonment as continuing presence. These are important elements of the experience of the persistence of presence. It is to re-cast an 'other' archaeological profile upon some of our 'treasured' archaeological tropes. It is to re-sensitize these tropes.

Profiling retains the intimacy of excavation, but goes beyond it to resonate directly with specific past situational memories. Through the use of context-specific scenarios, a theatricality of excavation (cf. Moshenska and Schadla-Hall 2011; Moshenska 2013; Hamilakis and Theou 2013) can afford new forms of archaeological life to emerge.

~John G. Sabol~

<u>Experiment, Excavation, Experience:</u>
<u>The 'Other' Side of Digging</u>

"The ruin must somehow manage to convey the notion...that the ancients who lived there might come back this very night and renew possession" (Tilden 1957:102).

"In theory, almost every person who lived in America left behind some trace of their passing...It is all there and we must not disregard it" (Deetz 1996:212).

Is this 'trace' merely 'things', as "things are the grounds of all archaeology" (Witmore 2017:232)? An archaeology that solely focuses its efforts, experience, and imagination on materiality is not regarding all that remains as equally important, while disregarding other presences of the past. Some practices of placemaking, still present today, remain as invisible qualities of presence. There are elements of human connections to space that are not readily apparent, leaving no 'marks', only sensory traces.

Excavation, as a form of 'etic' (and academic) 'habit memory' is productive-destructive interpretation at the trowel's edge. There are other performances, however, that can be practiced during the excavation process which can produce production from the destruction of physical

~John G. Sabol~

excavation that are not intrusive immersions while working with what remains of the past in the present. This becomes an acknowledgement of a form of presence, a form of life, usually excluded from the work of interpretative 'archaeologiness'.

Can a research process (performance experimentation) during a field methodology (excavation) produce a sensorial experience of the past in the present? Can objectively controlled conditions provide (afford) a subjective encounter that uncovers (recovers) knowledge of past conditions and situations? Can a worthwhile state, as a rite of passage to 'archaeologiness', be performed in a liminal position between experiment and experience, between archaeologist as participant-observer, and the presence of the past as producers of knowledge?

The space(s) of fieldwork matter. Particular spaces within landscapes are important historical artifacts, based on their marking of stability rather than ruin. The destruction of space through excavation is distressing because "stories cling to place...the fear is that stories will fly away unanchored, memory will dim, emotion will fade, identity will become tenuous if the geographical root is cut" (Kent Ryden).

Certain presences will remain hidden or, if exposed, remain unacknowledged. This becomes a concern for the 'witnessing' trace, the specter of re-narrations of the past as percolating, sensory materializations. If the "past somehow speaks for itself', let us at least acknowledge it when we experience it.

These traces do not emerge (except as 'residual' presence) from the earth so much as they are produced and become present through historical (and ethnographic) 'emic'-oriented performative experiments. This means a more immediate, intimate, and personal way of (really) working with what remains of the past in the present.

Experimenting with performance practices affords a sensorial impact on space and material culture which stresses an emotional engagement with attached spatial memories as surfacing profiles of presence. Such an approach, a "humanistic experimental archaeology" (Petersson and Narmo 2011), is an "action-mediated" methodology that can free archaeological 'habit memory' "from the control need, the need for repetition, in favor of individual approaches" (Ibid: 34).

This action-mediated methodology involves a particular sense of an archaeological site in which spaces are still 'active' and becoming present. As a result, the archaeological record is an eventful one, and its excavation has more to do with affording the emergence of potential presences, rather than knowing solely what physically remains as one excavates.

Holdorf (2017) has argued "that archaeology has ceased to be the discipline par excellence of things and material culture" (2017:187). This is due because "bodily sensations and evocative narratives are substituting for tangible evidence and hands-on experiments" (Ibid: 187). Archaeology today, "is about experiencing the past itself, face-to-face" (2017:187). But this 'experiencing', I propose is not a matter of provoking moments that entertain a temporal connection. It is not experiential coincidence or intentional 'rushes' (such as re-enactment 'wargasms').

It is the use of particular practices during the excavation process that produce social affordances ('actants') that result in sensorial materializations from the past. This 'past' is not "of a certain degree of pastness which is the contemporary quality of something to be 'of the past'" (2017:183). It is the presence of sensorial remains that endure. It is a particular 'timely' sensory profile of embedded or attached memory.

Experiments in performance practices and subjective experiences within percolating, though ephemeral, sensory elements is 'excavating' closer to a specific duration of time and memory entanglement. It contains a 'place in time' that is meaningful, a remembered 'thing' that continues to linger as a form of 'extended emotion' or "mindscape" (Sumyer Yu 2015). This 'mindscape' includes "mental data storage of scents, colors, sounds, temperatures, and meteorological patterns, all of which originate from human lived experiences enveloped in the external physical environment" (2015:20).

Is this part of what Tilley (2011) characterizes as a world entering the present through "a visionscape, a touchscape, a soundscape, a smellscape, and a tastescape"? This 'mindscape' can remain embedded, I propose, in the archaeological record. It may continue to surface today, but non-context-specific archaeological interventions can disturb or erase its presence. If so, we must be (become) conscious of this possible sensorial and ecological dimension, and the effects of non-conformity to it. Once experienced and acknowledged, we must re-act accordingly, and not 'rebury' it into the past.

~John G. Sabol~

'Excavating' into the Rhythms of Duration

Do multiple 'living' durations co-exist in the archaeological record? Are these "discrete temporalities incapable of attaining homogeneity with or full incorporation into a uniform chronological present" (Lim 2009:12)? Such durational entanglements within archaeological space, if they exist <u>and</u> percolate, would represent an ephemeral sensing of other past times (as duration) still present.

James Dixon (2012) has called such temporal disruptions "durational archaeologies" (2012:43). Such ephemerality of experienced time is a means to experience presence in a particular 'timely' way. It would alter the 'archaeologiness' of 'habit memory' excavations, a focus on the typical archaeologically visible. Excavations would, then, also be able to 'unearth' present-past durational acts still attached to the archaeological record.

An acceptance of the possibility of these ephemeral durations is to treat such materializations as a form of 'eventful archaeology', celebrating persistent rhythmic duration, rather than archaeology's recovery of embedded material remains. It is also to understand how things were (are) performed. After all, it is time, not the past, re-occurring. The primary medium of archaeological interest,

~John G. Sabol~

its object of concern, must be this human-initiated duration, not merely (only) the human past.

Should we think of the archaeological record as the duration of fields of memory: an "ever-accumulating ontological memory" (Lim 2009:15)? This requires going beyond the 'turn' (such as the 'turn to things'; the turn to...), and interpretations at the edge of a probing trowel. We must go beyond a horizon of sameness, the habits and rhythms of physically excavating a site, according to our perceptions of physical stratigraphy.

Let's begin to use field practices that can unearth the uncanny different. In his book, *Time and Free Will,* Henri Bergson (1889(2001)) states that space knows no duration, only simultaneity. In archaeological space, I propose, there is no time difference. Let's make this work for us during the dig, through bodily performances that simulate past rhythms of occupation within profiles of percolating memory.

Excavation becomes, not solely a measurement of incremental positions on a line, the starting and end points on a movement of time. It evolves into the interval between the unearthing and the measurement: the social interval of rhythm that connects the present to a duration that is present. This duration is not a 'life form' or a 'ghost' but an enduring 'form of life' still attached to a particular rhythmic profile of timeless space.

~John G. Sabol~

Neglecting or dismissing this possibility is what haunts contemporary (and past) excavations of the archaeological record. It is a refusal to complement the traditional narrative, populating it with subjective experience. With such a reality, the site report remains unfinished, an incomplete archaeological experience that will not endure into the future of archaeological exploration.

~John G. Sabol~

<u>*Performancescape:*</u>

<u>*A Return to Depth on the Surface*</u>

Archaeology is inherently performative fieldwork, but can archaeologists, during a penetrating surface 'excavation', become a performance of roles and tasks on a stage (the 'site') where social behavior (as "doings") becomes a critical part of fieldwork? This is not a form of 'performance archaeology', an 'emic' tint to a contemporary audience. It involves the physicality of performance, as context-specific rhythms of behavior on the basis of a series of engagements with material things, features, and spaces. These are 'affording' states to those ephemeral, ethnographic moments that materialize during fieldwork.

Is the archaeological record actually partially composed of an 'audience' observing? Such 'archaeological imagination' requires us to define 'who' is doing the observing, and what they are looking at as archaeologists perform fieldwork. It is not us, as archaeologists, observing and recording. It is us, as participants in moments of duration, not unearthing physical stratigraphy, but rather performing to profiles of embedded "social stratigraphy" (cf. Dawdy 2016): executing performance practices to attached memories.

Michael Shanks (2012) has said this:

~John G. Sabol~

Archaeology "deals in a past which is not so much over and done, no longer present, as both present in ruins and remains and uncanny non-absent phantoms, hauntingly present" (2012:148).

Are these 'phantoms' the durational, ethnographic moments when a profile of embedded memory materializes? An archaeological record, "pregnant with the past", may be full of these 'ghosts'. Traces abound on the surface, 'percolating' sensually, both ephemeral and repetitive, between darkness and exposure.

Is the role of archaeology merely to describe the 'ghostly' assemblages of things in a site's biography that have become exposed based on a pre-site objective? Does it 'haunt' particular periods as a form of fragmented material definition? Surely, it seems to offer little dynamic in exposing 'forms of life', beyond these descriptive narratives?

Is "new materialism" (cf. Witmore 2014) absent the real 'ghosts', those 'forms of life' still hauntingly present? Does it flatten the world of the past to the edge of a trowel, at the point of an objective (framed by academic constraints)? What about those surfacing profiles of presences from multiple pasts that remain unspoken about in 'official' reports? Still, they continue to percolate as ephemeral durations and cultural markers.

These materializations certainly do require a particular form of 'excavation' to separate and distinguish between layers of memory. This form of excavation becomes an extraction within context-specific performances, not the trowel, in order to gauge the reality of human duration in the archaeological record. Performance is essential for us to afford an archaeological knowledge of that plurimediated reality.

This is not the same as excavating a feature (even a burial). It is not repeating the actions in particular structural poses which echo those of the original setting (cf. Lucas 2001). This is because the contemporary social context, its performance, is not in rhythm with these durational profiles. Performance must be (afford) a socially-affecting meaning-making tool, and it must not impose – haunt. It must witness.

The archaeologist must become a co-performer who digs with, not digs out, the presence of the past at a site. This deflates the status and position of the archaeologist as the sole extractor of information about what past presence is recoverable and recovered. During the excavation process, the archaeologist becomes a participant-observer with the occupation(s) of the past, its fragmented, durational quality, and not a 'witness' to the visual absence revealed through excavation. It also means opening-up the interpretants of presence in the archaeological record as more than archaeologists. For example, there might exist distinct histories (durational episodes) of practices in the archaeological record. These result in very similar archaeological 'signatures' (Cipolla 2013).

We must unchain the semiotic grip of 'archaeologiness'. We must develop a framework whose baseline is thinking about being, and becoming present. This is not a view of static, dead 'life forms', but rather still active interpretants, as 'forms of life' emerging during the excavation process. 'Excavating' improvisational performances, in which a 'script' is created in the moment of materialization, can lead to discovery and uncanny outcomes (cf. Peters 2009).

Performances must go beyond the archaeological imagination toward imaginative practices in which social affordances are used to extract possible attached profiles of durational presence. Such performances, along with ruins and material culture, keep us in a past mood. Excavation, many times, keeps us out. This is because most excavations perform a different type of 'collective forgetting'. Its 'etic' focus into the past can suppress and purposely breakdown 'emic' rhythms of duration. This attaches a connection of fear to the link between the present and what endures in the archaeological record. Let us just become more 'emically-sensitive' to those uncanny durations of the presence of the past.

~John G. Sabol~

"Sounding-Out" 'Atmospheres' in the Record of Duration:

Translation or Transduction?

"The way we experience a space is determined largely by our aural perception and our physical presence within that space. Or our imagined projection of ourselves into that space".

- Christine McCombe 2001:64

There is a long, non-linear narrative of the ways that the past 'speaks' to us after history buries it. Archaeology is one of many means that unearths this twisting genealogy. But does the past really 'speak'? Have we, as archaeologists, become too enculturally-blinded by the visual presence of the past to largely ignore other mediums of presence? Have our translations been merely focused on the many ocular forms of this presence? What if *'kairos'* (or actuality), as the conjunction of two or more times, is not only a vision of material remains, but also the transduction of duration by other sensory modalities, such as sound?

~John G. Sabol~

Are there "sound artifacts" (Benjamin 2014) in the archaeological record? Are they "a recognizable, repeatable, reproductive sound made by people, other life forms…one that endures through time, with negligible variability" (2014:120)? Are these agentic today? Such a possibility would define place, and its archaeological record, as something not bounded by space but defined by sound.

How does one quantify a normally-observed spatial absence? The archaeological record is not 'muted' by the perception of pastness or the lack of sensorial remains. It is 'silenced' by the assumed absence of non-visual modalities (cf. Denardi 2013).

"Because everything engages sound, sound acts to link and collectivize bodies and environments, creating different kinds of atmospheres" (Gallagher et.al. 2016:9).

Are these 'atmospheres' embedded in the archaeological record? Are they records of duration: 'recording profiles' that remain attached in archaeological space? Do they also act as forms of environmental affordances that bind presences to particular spaces in layers of memory? Does this entangle contemporary humans (such as archaeologists), past (attached) presences, animals, objects, technologies, and the environment in chains of association across spatial-durational time?

Does the recording of these remains require particular "timework" practices? Do these sounds disrupt common spatialities, perceptions, archaeological/academic politics, and material presences? Does this disruption go beyond the trowel's destructive nature and its visual line of inquiry? Can it reveal different aspects of sensorial space amid ruin and absence? Can sound create durational "acoustic arenas" (Blesser and Salter 2007)? Given the priority ('archaeologiness') of traditional excavation that favors depth to surface, layers of ground to those of memory, and visual presence, the search for sonic elements requires more sensitivity to the craft of listening as part of the craft of archaeological fieldwork.

Does a socially-affective 'atmosphere' of certain past occupations (such as battlefields) remain embedded in particular spaces? Are affective qualities "autonomous from the bodies that they emerge from, enable, and perish with" (Anderson 2009:80), or are they an outcome of attached memories of a still 'active' presence? If sounds act to link and collectivize bodies and environments, creating different kinds of atmospheres (Gallagher et.al. 2016:9), are there certain atmospheres afforded by archaeological excavation? Are they constructive or destructive to the presences of the past?

Can we record these different kinds of atmospheres? Do some represent "non-cochlear" (Kim-Cohen 2009) sonic geographies, sensed and heard through the skin and within bodily cavities and organs (such as a form of past infrasound)? Is this a vestigial artifact, a presence that is both contemporary and the past? The recording of these presences becomes an archaeology of a usually hidden aural record, one that might materialize ever so ephemerally in survey and excavation. Do they represent a surfacing memory flash, triggered by human behavior (both past and present)?

This possibility provides an expanded ethno-archaeological presence. It results in a different understanding of the present. It gives archaeology an alternative message beyond its traditional spatial and temporal parameters of 'archaeologiness'.

Archaeological work is usually perceived as an intellectual exercise in vision through the trope of an archaeological gaze, of the seen through remote and penetrating technologies, survey walking, and physical excavation. These are interpretations at the edge of the visible and the visual. Can it also be an excavation through sound, a transduction of the medium of recovery toward the sights and sounds of the past in the present?

The appearance of sound 'remains' acknowledges the complexity of a pluri-mediated past, even amid ruin, trace, and fragmentation. Can excavations be guided, and knowledge produced, by the sensory experience afforded by digging (other than the visual turn of the trowel) to a turn toward these sounds? Can listening become as important as hearing about how we can accomplish our rite of passage as archaeologists through the trope of 'archaeologiness'?

What Else Matters?

'Interstitial' Archaeology: Can We Frame the 'Out of Frame' Context In a Way that Matters?

Alejandro Haber (2013) has said this about fieldwork:

"During investigation surprising things happen and if we pay attention to them, they lead us to unforeseen and new situations. ..In addition, things happen at the margins of our sight during investigation, things to which we can only pay attention if we switch our attention towards places different to the foreseen ones" (2013:87).

Can we excavate a site as a way of sensing the past, an awareness that important actions may take place out of the normal frame of excavation? These become, not an interpretation at the trowel's edge, but at a visionary, sensory edge. Are some archaeological spaces "parafunctional spaces" (Hayward 2012): an abandoned, normally absent presence that manifests out of the frame of 'archaeologiness'?

A perceived empty landscape is not a "surfaceless space" (Schmitz 2014). It is an atmospheric field of situations and potentialities. This is because the strongest metaphor of archaeology, as a discipline that studies what is dead (Gonzales-Ruibal 2013:21), may not be the only operational reality in fieldwork.

In *Sinister Resonance,* David Toop (2010) discusses Charles Dickens' 1862 novel *Haunted House:*

"If we believe what we cannot see, we cannot know, then the possibility exists that inert and lifeless objects may have a secret life that only reveals itself when we look away or fall asleep" (Toop 2010:126).

During fieldwork, do we sometimes miss this "secret life" opportunity? Do we distance knowledge by distinguishing a past, the archaeological present, as everything that only happens in front of our eyes? Are we 'blinded', and side-tracked, by a material culture that is only verifiable by "Western canons of evidence"? Can we look laterally beyond "mythistory" (Mali 2003) toward an 'ethnophenomenology'?

If presence means social experience, rather than material culture, can an enduring human presence be thought of as "the name of a relation, of a position in relation to other possible positions" (Vivieros de Castro 1998)? Can it be experienced as parallel surface percolations, rather than excavation depth? Does it make the surface 'haunted' by underexposure?

Archaeology, rather than simply being the study, analysis, and interpretation of material culture, is itself a performance practice of the between. It is the interstitial art of making and unmaking of different past realities and other than human presences and materialities that are their source and agency in the present. Might not different decisions, performances as opposed to habit memory practices, reveal a different world at the edge of assumed reality? Is this more than constructing imaginative horizons?

If archaeology is about memory, why is it so focused and enthusiastic about contemporary technological advancements that uncover hidden ruin and rubble? Why do archaeologists get excited about a ruin technology of absence? Why not develop performance practices and technologies to recover the absent presences of the ephemeral, the durational, the still percolating uncanny. It is these embedded and attached traces of past sensoriums, as forms of life that also matter. Is ethno-phenomena one lighted path out of the 'Black Holes' of excavation? Can we make it matter?

~John G. Sabol~

Ethno-Phenomena:

'Percolations' that Matter?

Excavation alone does not unearth all that remains. We know that. But does it unearth what remains of the past through contemporary 'etic' fieldwork? In the 1950's, M.A. Smith (1955) insisted that there is no "necessary link" between what remains and "the human activity we should like to know about". Four decades later, Julian Thomas (1996) has said that "archaeology requires us to make the world static to freeze it in order to interpret it" (1996:63).

Are these 'frozen' remains past activity? How can we say so, if the past still percolates in the present? What are we interpreting at the trowel's edge: a frozen wasteland, a 'lifeless' space? Where is our 'emic' sensitivity to what remains? What is there between the hidden and the percolating field? Are we still imaginatively ill-defining the past? What lies beyond the spade, the trowel, and the LIDAR?

Is there still an 'emic' presence of human activity in the archaeological record? Is it a presence that affords "historically-situated agency" (Robb 2010:499) of particular social situations?

"The ghost is not simply a dead or missing person, but a social figure" (Gordon 1997:8).

~John G. Sabol~

111

Is this 'ghost' the human activity that is still percolating in the present? Is it ontologically valid, or is it a misperception, a trick of the archaeological imagination? Is this the darkness of destruction or something else?

~John G. Sabol~

Excavations into Darkness

Does it matter when we excavate? Does the light of day obstruct the presence of certain past presence? Does working (and performing) in the dark as a form of sensory deprivation actually recover something of the presence of embedded and still attached 'human activity'? Do 'excavating' performances at night avoid much of the sensory 'noise' of the day? Are there traces of cultural realms that can be explored right there and then (in the dark) without labeling it "ghost hunting"?

The dark challenges the once privileged position of the observer over the subject of observation. This ocular 'blurring' actually allow us to become more sensually attentive to non-visual cues. Between present subject and past object, a sense of experience becomes a 'digging' tool. It crosses ('excavates') through conventional time ('archaeological stratigraphy') and observed space (ruin, objects, and features). It pushes forward the surface toward possible percolating, 'emic' encounters.

Darkness can mean many things. But is it a sense-filled intervention? In a recent book, *Archaeology of the Night* (Gonlin and Nowell 2017), the authors explore the archaeological signatures of nighttime behaviors. They suggest that we reimagine sites "through the dark lens of the night to explore the past". In fieldwork, we rarely experience the site at night, except perhaps as a contemporary social interaction.

The excavation of the 'night past' that is advocated here, however, does not draw on the 'usual suspects' of material culture. It concerns embedded sensory remains of nighttime activities, or to those activities attached to objects used at night. Does this 'nighttime sensory culture' still haunt the archaeological record? If humans live in ecological rather than geological time, can we immerse ourselves in 'excavating' performances context-specific to layers of memory that are associated with the night?

This would extend an excavation experientially to interpretations of performance practices at the edge of darkness. This would go beyond the daylight hours into the night. Fieldwork would become, in these practices a 'simming' of past 'nightscapes' by modifying our rhythms toward nocturnal human activity.

These night 'excavations' negate the idea "that the past is entirely separate from the present". If archaeology is about memory and the presence of the past in the present, let's be fully conscious of our timely interventions. This involves exploring the ecological dimensions of occupation both during the day and at night. It means that the site need not be accessed in a particular way:

"Archaeology must also rethink some of its basic notions of what constitutes archaeological material, the conditions for how to approach or know this material, and the prospects

~John G. Sabol~

for what should be the outcome of that effort" (Petursdottir and Olsen 2017:12).

A focus remains on the human shadows that endure through time, and whose sensory 'footprint' may be obscured by the 'daylight' of archaeological excavation.

~John G. Sabol~

'Haunted Dirt':

What May Matter is 'Out of Sight'?

"The ground is no less important than the objects we find in it".

- Andre Leroi (1950:11)

Digging destroys the socially-affording contexts of the past. Does it matter? Apparently not, for most archaeologists. Digging is the rite of passage that transforms an empty ground to an archaeological site through the 'archaeologiness' of exposing what lies under the dirt and debris.

Digging might be viewed as an "abduction" (Gell 1998) of agency. Digging represents how the present still affects the past, how the archaeological record continues to be transformed. Yet, "those with the privilege of doing archaeology as a profession are challenged by the narrowness of their experiences" (Cunningham and MacEachearn 2016).

Has exposed dirt become 'haunted' because of its removal? Is it now out of context, a social 'mess'? Has excavation produced "presence effects" through the removal of certain layers of ground as insignificant to the objective at hand? Does this removal affect particular presences and states of being, such as environmentally embedded ('residual') presence?

Barrett (2016) has said this:

"What will it take for archaeologists to operate not as if its role were to interpret the representation of the past but to engage with that part of the reality of the past that exists today" (2016:135).

Is part of that 'presence' reality a form of life embedded in and attached to that 'dirt'? Is it the messy ground, as the gap between "the lived past, and its ruin today" (Shanks 1992)? Have excavations by-passed the liminal states of 'embeddedness' and 'attachment' in percolating durational fields of memory? Are most archaeologists digging past it because it is not object-oriented ground?

Is this 'haunted ground', a matter of loss and archaeological forgetting, really the 'right stuff', even "vibrant matter" (Bennett 2010) and something that does matter? Is this ignored presence, not a matter 'out of time', "not a record of their absence" (Barrett 2016:135)? Is it rather a presence that confronts and confounds the concept of absence in archaeological field reports? Is this 'haunting' more than a metaphor for the 'etic' medium (excavation) of fieldwork? Is object-centered excavation a feature-filled mode of forgetting, or a purposeful ignoring of uncanny experiences?

~John G. Sabol~

Out of the destructive nature of excavation, can come a new meaning to the perception of presence and the duration of fragments of the past in the present. Anthropologist Gaston Gordillo (2013) has shown that "to rethink the concept of 'the ruin' through the social and affective reconfigurations created by traces of destruction" (2013:324) can create these new meanings.

Do 'ghosts' of ignored presence sit in the space of ignored and discarded dirt, in landscapes scarred (and scared) by archaeological excavation? Is this ground, a dearth of dirty mess, part of the landscape that is "pregnant with the past"? Why is it not included in an extended, still materializing and transforming, archaeological record?

If the archaeological medium does not include working with this past dirt, then forgotten messages of past presence, cleared by survey and excavation, are clearly lost. How 'clear' of interpretation is this archaeological 'sweep'? Are we missing something in the process of clearing the ground, ordering the mess to our contemporary archaeological standards by merely scanning the visual exposures?

Are we in danger of losing our now long established perspective on documenting the presences of the past because we continue to restrict our archaeological reality? What other narratives of the past can be derived from the mess, the 'afterlife' of clearance? What are the conditions, approaches, and prospects in re-evaluating this messy ground?

~John G. Sabol~

If time and space are cultural artifacts (cf. Kern 1983), then what sensually remains, transcending both, must be anchored to a particular layer (and profile) of ground. Does space and time, as artifacts of discarded ground, contain sounds and smells that anchor them to a particular profile of cultural memory? Let's make sensory sense of that mess!

~John G. Sabol~

Mess Also Matters:

'Vibrancy' in Debris

In the fragmented landscapes in which archaeologists work, practices associated with surface and layered underground spaces and structures and notions of detritus, can create entangled disorder. This contextual 'mess is integral to the "affective' (Stewart 2011) presence of 'archaeologiness'. Archaeological field performances that organize this messy collection is a form of 'placemaking'. It creates assemblages that gather ideas of landscape stories.

But are these the only stories? Is this creation of organized 'mess' the only alternative in a bounded performance of 'archaeologiness'? Is there also an imagination playground for those seekers of the uncanny? Might this uncanny also bring order to the archaeological landscape mess?

Can an archaeological attunement to such uncanny mess, though ephemeral, create matters of importance? If archaeology is not always about the way something looks, or how this look can be reconstructed, then the mess can create an alternative re-remembering of place. The fragmentary landscape in ruin constitutes a different 'spectral turn' of forgotten memory.

This is not "matter out of place" (Douglas 1968) in archaeology because presence may be attached, remaining

~John G. Sabol~

in place as something still commanding affect and affordance. The visible fields of absent human presence are not really devoid of the presence of human memory, even though they may be centuries old. Hidden from sight are surface 'bunkers' of myth, producing myth-making possibilities.

The ordering of messy mythic spaces can create a 'haunted' landscape, a type of heritage in the making. It is a form of re-telling the past that frequently has been lost and forgotten, in locations where the "histories that cannot rest" (Coddington 2011) continue to percolate in the present. Re-surfacing, percolating, fragmented histories represent the presence of an alternative landscape (Vergunst 2012).

This is a landscape not normally in archaeological view, but one still indicative of the presence of the past, still becoming present. It surfaces without the aid of intrusive archaeological excavation, the surfacing reminds us today of the futility of separating the past from the present, affect and atmosphere, and the living from the dead. We must never define an abandoned landscape as absent a continuing presence. It means that the mess of what's present can be affectively archaeologically significant.

~John G. Sabol~

<u>And so...........</u>

A 'Final Dig' at/in Archaeology

In our exposure of traces and fragments, as synechdocal excavation, are we missing (ignoring) other (past social) contexts? Are we merely interpreting 'metaphorically', taking the representation of what we physically uncover for an adequate sample represented? Is excavation, as 'habit memory', an unearthing of the 'usual suspects' ('things' as assemblages of material culture)? Are our passions during digging merely a reflection of the traditional archaeological way of "doings": a collector's chaos made to order?

Did Walter Benjamin refer to archaeological excavation when he said: "for what else is this collection but a disorder to which habit has accommodated itself to such an extent that it can appear as order"? Is this order a modernist (etic) version of understanding and interpreting what an excavation might (should) uncover?

Archaeology provides its researchers an uncanny experience, working in landscapes of ruin, the recovery of absent presence. This experience is still tempered, however, by little past ethnographic sensorial flavoring, being bounded by professional contemporary bonding realities (the 'archaeologiness' of the profession).

~John G. Sabol~

That past in the present that is encountered and experienced, at times elevated both close and vivid, is rarely vibrant, a social experience when working with what remains. Those non-uncanny immersions involve more a 'team spirit' than a 'spirited' encounter of past occupational spaces.

Still, the archaeologist, in a relational entanglement with past space and material culture, has an opportunity as "having-been-there" (Barthes 1977:44). Laurent Olivier (2011) has stated that "there is no way to restore the past" (2011:48). Yet, some sensory elements of the past have not past. Have 'YOU' experienced them? Some percolate, without intervention, in the present.

These environmental residues can be thought of as "topographies of remembrance" (Wood 2013). Is this 'profile imprinting' part of the "formation processes" (Schiffer 1987) of a site's archaeological record? Why are these seldom reported as having been experienced during fieldwork?

The fairy tale that beings with "Once upon a time" can become present, if only for an ephemeral duration, and repeatable during fieldwork. Are these what Gerard Choquer (2004) calls "morphological hysteresis": a dormant period that suddenly becomes 'active'? Is it waiting for an archaeological intervention, or does it require more work when working with what remains of the past? Is there an "emotional authenticity" (cf. Bagnall 2003) needed to experience this presence during fieldwork to have an effect on us?

Why are we not citing this experience in a report? Is it because it doesn't happen or is this a lack of professional responsibility toward the past present? If the archaeological record contains layers of memory, attached to sensory elements, it creates a "relational aesthetics" (Bourriaud 2004) that encourages "moments of sociability" (Bourriaud 1998:33).

Historically, there has always been multiple representations of reality: from a flat world to a flat ontology, to a flattened surface assemblage, or a 'flattened' time, the way in which the past is manifesting in the present. There are the stories surrounding old abandoned buildings and ruins where their physical attributes, in various stages of ruination, are imbued with "imaginary elements that strengthen their role in mythological thought" (Yentsch 1988:11).

This can led to superficial, archaeologically-influenced surveys into "ruin-porn" through photographic exposures and urban exploration. The images portrayed and experiences encountered in these places can possess "material agency and produce destabilizing affects affording the imagining of haunting anthropomorphic figures to animate the landscape' (Manning 2017:64).

But can we today break into the 'sense' barrier of archaeological non-sensed interventions, after experiencing an 'uncanny' recognition? Can we do this without feeling it being nonsense? Can we not only react to it, but also include the experience in a site report?

An alternative to representation is to think of realism in terms of cultural intervention: what counts as real is what we can affect or what affects us (Hacking 1983:146), as we perform with specific cultural practices of re-occupation attuned to a particular profile of memory.

From its inception as a field disciplinary practice, archaeology was an exercise in imagination, but "the question of what archaeology is may most convincingly be answered by those who are doing it, but it is only verifiable as such by those who one day will have done something else" (Burstein 2004:124).

Archaeology is not just about being an archaeologist and doing what is required of them ("archaeologiness"). Part of that something else is doing something in the form of alternative pathways that affect or afford a sensory, rather than material, presence of the past in the present. It is what Michael Herzfeld calls "uncanny recognitions" (2012:54).

Archaeology is a lively journey on a never ending (not final) road to the past in the present. Archaeologists interact with, and impact, this "world in production" that is the transforming presence of the past. The journey contains multiple ways of knowing, forever percolating in text and method, as presences, theory, and fieldwork models come and go.

~John G. Sabol~

It becomes "a caravan: a heterogeneous ensemble of ideas and methods on the move" (Conquergood 1995:140). The habitual tropes of archaeological practices, however, certainly remain and represent forms of 'trespasses' on the lives of the past. Thus, archaeology must become more experience-based, not as a rite of passage toward an archaeological career, but to a humanity that still percolates where archaeologists continue to dig.

Mortimer Wheeler said long ago:

"In a simple direct sense, archaeology is a science that must be lived, must be seasoned with humanity. Dead archaeology is the driest dust that blows" (from *Archaeology from the Earth,* 1954).

On the surface of our record of archaeological occupation and intervention, this sense of humanity, as a past human sensorium, still largely remains 'buried'. We still haven't fully experienced the rhythmic sensorial entanglement of duration during our fieldwork interventions:

"The ground is all memoranda and signatures, and every object covered over with hints" (Ralph Waldo Emerson, 1850).

Let's stop avoiding these other 'signatures', and take these 'hints' from a still percolating past!

~John G. Sabol~

Appendix:

My 'Rite of Passage' into 'Archaeologiness'

I began my professional archaeological training at Winchester (UK) in 1969. According to John Collis, "no one excavation had a greater impact on archaeology in Britain in the later twentieth century than Martin Biddle's project in Winchester in the 1960's" (2011:74). So, I had a 'great' introduction to that 'rite of passage' into 'archaeologiness'. At Winchester:

- "a new diachronic vision" was born;
- "new approaches to excavation, such as open area, metrication, and the matrix approach to stratigraphical analysis" was begun; and a
- "model" for the professional 'units', which now dominate British archaeology" began (Ibid: 74).

At Winchester, my work centered on Wolvesey Palace. My specific excavating centered on

<u>Photos 1-6: The Winchester 'Experience:</u>

<u>Photo 1: Wolvesey Palace (1969)</u>

<u>*Photo 2: Wolvesey Palace (1969)*</u>

<u>*Photo 3: Wolvesey Palace (1969)*</u>

<u>*Photo 4: Within the Walls of Wolvesey Palace (1969)*</u>

<u>Photo 5: The Layers of Strata (1969)</u>

~John G. Sabol~

Photo 6: My Excavation Space (1969)

~John G. Sabol~

Photo 7: My Excavation Space (1969)

~John G. Sabol~

Photo 8: Home (Near the Cathedral~ 1969)

From Winchester, I continued my archaeological 'rite of passage' the following season in Mexico. Specifically, I attended a field school at the University of the Americas in Cholula, Mexico for 12 weeks.

<u>*Photos 9-13: The Cholula 'Experience'*</u>

<u>*Photo 9: 'Digging-Deep (1970)*</u>

Photo 10: The Archaeological Grid (1970)

~John G. Sabol~

<u>*Photo 11: The Archaeological Grid (1970)*</u>

Photo 12: The Archaeological Grid (1970)

Photo 13: Encountering the Past – with Dr. Joseph Mountjoy (1970)

~John G. Sabol~

Photo 14: The View from the Site (1970)

At Winchester and Cholula, did my participation into professional 'archaeologiness' dig sensibly and sensitively into the archaeological record of those landscapes, providing an opportunity for an 'emic' perspective to emerge? Was the work a positive inscription or a negative erasure (and destruction)? Only 'durations' of memory will tell, only future archaeological presence will 'speak' to that.

This is the archaeological dilemma: how has one's interventions affected the presences of the past? Have they afforded a positive impact on the present and future occupations of the landscapes, places, and spaces we excavate? The future of archaeology will tell that story.....

~John G. Sabol~

<u>*Bibliography*</u>

Abbas, Ackbar.   1994. Building on Disappearance. *Public Culture 6:*441-459.

Anderson, B. 2009. Affective Atmospheres. *Emotion, Space and Society* 2 (2): 77-81.

Appadurai, Arjun.   1986. Introduction: Commodities and the Politics of Value in the Social Life of Things in *The Social Life of Things: Commodities in Cultural Perspective. Arjun Appadurai (Editor).* New York: Cambridge University Press. pp. 3-63.

Arnold, Bettina. 1999. The Contested Past. *Anthropology Today* 15 (4): 1-4.

Arojona, Jamie M. 2015. Sublime Perversions: Capturing the Uncanny Affects of Queer Temporalities in Mississippian Ruins. *Journal of Social Archaeology* Volume 16 (2): 189-215.

Ashmore, Wendy and Robert Sharer. 2000. *Discovering Our Past: A Brief Introduction to Archaeology.* New York: McGraw-Hill.

Bagnall, G. 2003. Performance and Performativity at Heritage Sites. *Museum and Society* 1 (2): 87-103.

Bailey, D. 2017. Art and Archaeology. *One World Archaeology* 11. I.A. Russell, A. Cochrane (Editors). pp. 231-250.

2017. Disarticulate-RePurpose-Disrupt: Art/Archaeology. *Cambridge Archaeological Journal* 4 (27): 691-701.

Bakhtin, M.M. 1981. *The Dialogic Imagination.* C. Emerson and M. Holquist (Translation). Austin: University of Texas Press.

Barrett, John. 1988. The Living, the Dead, and the Ancestors: Neolithic and Early Bronze Age Mortuary Practices in *The Archaeology of Context in the Neolithic and Bronze Age: Recent Trends.* John Barrett and Ian Kinnes (Editors). Sheffield: Sheffield Academic Press. pp. 30-41.

2016. Archaeology after Interpretation: Returning Humanity to Archaeological Theory. *Archaeological Dialogues* 26 (2): 133-137.

Barthes, Roland. 1977. *A Lover's Discourse.* Richard Howard (Translation). London: Vintage.

Basso, Keith H. 1984. Stalking with Stories: Names, Places, and Moral Narratives among the Western Apache in *Text, Play, and Story: The Construction and Reconstruction of Self and Society.* Washington, D.C.: American Ethnological Society. pp. 19-55.

Bauer, Alexander. 2013. Objects and their Glassy Essence: Semiotics of Self in the Early Bronze Age Black Sea. *Signs and Society 1 (1):* 1-31.

Beisaw, April. 2016. Ghost Hunting as Archaeology, Archaeology as Ghost Hunting in *Lost City, Found Pyramid: Understanding Alternative Archaeologies and Pseudoscientific Practices.* Edited by Jeb J. Card and David S. Anderson. Tuscaloosa: University of Alabama press. pp. 185-198.

Bell, Catherine. 1997. *Ritual: Perspectives and Dimensions.* New York: Oxford University Press.

Bender, Barbara. 2002. Time and Landscape. *Current Anthropology* 43: S103-S112.

2007. *Stone Worlds: Narrative and Reflexivity in Landscape Archaeology.* Barbara Bender, Sue Hamilton, Chris Tilley (Editors). Walnut Creek, California: Left Coast Press, Inc.

Benjamin, Walter. 1932 (2003). *Selected Writings. Volume 4 (1938-1940).* Cambridge: Belknap Press.

Benjamin, Jeff. 2014. Sound as Artifact. MA Thesis (Department of Social Sciences). Michigan Technological University.

Bennett, Jane. 2010. *Vibrant Matter: A Political Ecology of Things.* Durham: Duke University Press.

Bergson, Henri. 1889 (2001). *An Essay on the Immediate Data of Consciousness. Translation by F.L. Pogson. Mineola, New York: Dover.*

Bierwert, Crisca. 1999. *Brushed by Cedar, Living by the River: Coast Salish Figures of Power.* Tucson: University of Arizona Press.

Bird-David, N. 1999. Animinism Re-Visited:Personhood, Environment, and Relational Epistemology. *Current Anthropology* 40: S67-S91.

Blesser, Barry and Linda-Ruth Salter. 2007. *Spaces Speak, Are You Listening? Experiencing Aural Architecture.* Cambridge: MIT Press.

Bourriaud, Nicholas. 1998. *Relational Aesthetics.* Les Presse du Reel, Franc.

2004. *Postproduction: Culture as Screenplay: How Art Reprograms the World.* Sternberg Press.

Bowser, Brenda J. and Maria Nieves Zedeno. 2009. *The Archaeology of Meaningful Places.* Edited by Brenda J. Bowser and Maria Nieves Zedeno. Salt Lake City: University of Utah Press.

Bradley, Robert. 2000. *An Archaeology of Natural Places.* London: Routledge.

Bridge, Gavin. 2013. Territory, Now in 3D! *Political Geography XXXIV/(6).*

Buccellati, Giorgio. 2017. *A Critique of Archaeological Reason: Structural, Digital, and Philosophical Aspects of the Excavated Record.* Cambridge: Cambridge University Press.

Burstein, Jessica. 2004. Infra-Dig: A Response to Gavin Lucas. *Modernism/Modernity* Volume 11 (1): 121-124.

Casey, E. S. 1987. *Remembering: A Phenomenological Study.* Bloomington, Indiana: Indiana University Press.

Castaneda, Quetzil. 1996. *In the Museum of Mayan Culture: Touring Chichen Itza.* Minneapolis: University of Minnesota Press.

Chard, Chloe. 1999. The Road to Ruin: Memory, Ghosts, Moonlight, and Weeds in *Roman presences: Receptions of Rome in European Culture 1789-1945.* Edited by Catherine Edwards. Cambridge, U.K.: Cambridge University Press. pp. 125-139.

Choquer, Gerard. 2004. Crise el Recomposition des Objets: Les Enjeux del Archeologie in Objets en crise, Objets Recomposes *Etudes Rurales* 167 (8): 13-32.

Cipolla, Craig. 2013. Native American History, Archaeology, and the Trope of Authenticity. *Historical Archaeology* 47 (3): 12-22.

Coddington, K.S. 2011. Spectral Geographies: Haunting and Everyday State Practices in Colonial and Present-day Alaska. *Social and Cultural Geography* 12 (7): 743-756.

Collis, John. 2011. The Urban Revolution: Martin Biddle's Excavations in Winchester, 1961-1971 in *Great Excavations: Shaping the Archaeological Profession.* John Schofield (Editor). Oxford: Oxbow. pp. 74-86.

Colwell-Chanthaphonb, Chip, T.J. Ferguson, and Roger Anyon. 2008. Always Multivocal and Multivalent: Conceptualizing Archaeological Landscape in Arizona's San Pedro Valley in *Archaeology of Placemaking: Monuments, Memories and Engagements in Native North America.* Patricia E. Rubertone (Editor). Walnut Creek, California: Left Coast Press, Inc. pp. 59-80.

Connerton, P. 2008. Seven Types of Forgetting. *Memory Studies* 1: 59-71.

Conquergood, D. 1995. Of Caravans and Carnivals: Performance Studies in Motion. *The Drama Review* 39 (4): 137-141.

Couclelis, H. 1992. People Manipulate Objects (but cultivate fields) Beyond the Raster-Vector Debate in GIS in A.U. Frank and I. Campari (Editors) *From Space to Territory: Theories and Methods of Spatio-Temporal Reasoning in Geographic Space. Springer-Verlag. Pp. 65-77.*

Crang, M. and P.S. Travlou. 2001. The City and Topographies of Memory. *Environment and Planning D: Society and Space* 19: 161-177.

Cresswell, Tim. 2003. *Place: A Short Introduction.* Blackwell.

Croissant, Jennifer L. 2014. Agnotology: Ignorance and Absence or Towards. *Social Epistemology* Volume 28 (No. 1): 4-25.

Crouch, David. 2010. Unravelling Space and Landscape in Leisure's Identities. *Landscapes of Leisure: 8-23.*

Cunningham, Jerimy and Scott MacEachern. 2016. Ethnography as Slow Science. *World Archaeology* Volume 48: 628-641.

Darvill, Timothy. 2015. Observation, Analogy, Experimentation and Rehabitation During Archaeological Excavations in *On Metaphorical How Do We Imagine the Past?* Edited by Dragos Gheorghiu and Paul Bouissac. Newcastle Upon Tyne, UK: Cambridge Scholars Publishing.

Dawdy, Shannon Lee. 2016. *Patina: A Profane Archaeology.* Chicago: University of Chicago Press.

DeCerteau, Michel. 1984. *The Practice of Everyday Life.* Berkeley: University of California Press.

Deetz, James. 1996. *In Small Things Forgotten: An Archaeology of Early American Life.*

Delaplace, Gregory. 2014. What the Invisible Looks Like: Ghosts, Perceptual Faith, and Mongolian Regimes of Communication in *The Social Life of Spirits.* Edited by Roy Blanes and Diana Espirito Santo. Chicago: University of Chicago Press. pp. 52-68.

DeLoria, Philip. 2006. What is the Middle Ground Anyway? *The William and Mary Quarterly* 63 (1): 15-22.

DeNardi, Sarah. 2012. How Natural are Natural Places? Challenging Stereotypes in the Interpretation of Landscape in Iron Age Veneto, Italy in *Place as Material Culture: Objects, Geographies, and the Construction of Time.* Edited by Dragos Gheopghiu and George Nash. pp.277-298.

2013. An Embodied Approach to Second World War Storytelling Mementoes: Probing Beyond the Archival into the Corporeality of Memories of the Resistance. *Journal of Material Culture* Volume 19 (4): 443-464.

Dening, Greg. 1996. *Performances.* Chicago: University of Chicago Press.

Derrida, J. 1994. *Specters of Marx: The State of Debt, the Work of Mourning, and the New International.* London: Routledge.

Dixon, James. 2012. Archaeological Explorations of Duration in the Contemporary City. *Performance Research: A Journal of the Performing Arts* 17 (5): 41-46.

Dorrian, Mark and Gillian Rose. 2003 (Editors). *Deterritorializations Revisioning: Landscapes and Politics.* Black Dog Publishing.

Douglas, Mary. 1966. *Purity and Danger: An Analysis of Concepts of Pollution and Taboo.* London: Routledge.

1968. Pollution in D. Sills (Editor) *International Encyclopedia of the Social Sciences.* pp. 336-341.

Edensor, T. and DeSilvey C. 2012. Reckoning with Ruins. *Progress in Human Geography.*

Edgeworth, Matt. 2011. Excavation as a Ground of Archaeological Knowledge. *Archaeological Dialogues* 18 (1): 44-46.

Eiseley, Loren. 1975. *All the Strange Hours: The Excavation of a Life.* New York: Charles Scribner's Sons.

Fagan, Brian. 1995. *Time Detectives: How Scientists Use Modern Technology to Unravel the Secrets of the Past.* New York: Simon and Schuster.

Ferrell, J. 2015. "Ghost Ethnography: On Crimes Against Reality and their Excavation". Paper presented at "Crimes Against Reality", University of Hamburg, Germany.

Flaherty, Michael G. 2011. *Agency and Temporal Experience.* Philadelphia: Temple University Press.

Fowles, S.M. 2013. *An Archaeology of Doings: Secularism and the Study of Pueblo Religion.* Santa Fe: School for Advanced Research Press.

Gallagher, M. et.al. 2016. Listening Geographies: Landscape, Affect, and Geotechnologies. M. Gallagher, Anja Kanngieser, Jonathan Prior. *Progress in Human Geography.* pp.1-20.

Gauvreau, Alisha and Duncan McLaren. 2016. Stratigraphy and Storytelling: Imbricating Indigenous Oral Narratives and Archaeology on the Northwest Coast of North America. *Hunter-Gatherer Research* pp. 303-325.

Gell, Alfred. 1998. *Art and Agency: An Anthropological Theory.* Oxford: Clarendon Press.

Geertz, Clifford. 1995. *After the Fact: Two Countries, Four Decades, One Anthropology.* Cambridge: Harvard University Press.

Ginsberg, Robert.   2004. *The Aesthetics of Ruins.* Amsterdam: Rodopi.

Gonlin, Nancy and April Nowell. 2017. *Archaeology of the Night: Life After Dark in the Ancient World.* Boulder: University Press of Colorado.

Gnecco, Cristobal. 2013. Digging Alternative Archaeologies in *Reclaiming Archaeology: Beyond the Tropes of Modernity.* Edited by Alfredo Gonzalez-Ruibal. London: Routledge. pp. 67-78.

Gonzalez-Ruibal, Alfredo.   2008. Time to Destroy: An Archaeology of Supermodernity. *Current Anthropology* 49 (2): 247-279.

2013. *Reclaiming Archaeology: Beyond the Tropes of Modernity.* Alfredo Gonzalez-Ruibal (Editor). London: Routledge.

2016. *Etica de la Hospitalidad.* Madrid: Peninsula.

Gordillo, Gaston. 2013. Bringing a Place in Ruins Back to Life in *Reclaiming Archaeology: Beyond the Tropes of Modernity.* Alfredo Gonzalez-Ruibal (editor). London: Routledge. pp. 323-336.

2014. *Rubble: The Afterlife of Destruction.* Durham: Duke University Press.

Gordon, Avery. 1997. *Ghostly Matters: Haunting and the Sociological Imagination.* Minneapolis: University of Minnesota Press.

Grady, Jill. 2011. Ancestors, Ethnohistorical Practice, and the Authentication of Native Place and Past in *Phantom Past, Indigenous Present: North American Ghosts in Native American Culture and History.* Edited by Colleen E. Boyd and Coll Thrush. Lincoln: University of Nebraska Press.

Graves-Brown, P. 2011. Archaeology: A Career in Ruins. *Archaeological Dialogues 18 (2): 168-171.*

Graves-Brown, P. Rodney Harrison, Angela Piccini. 2013. *The Oxford Handbook of the Archaeology of the Contemporary World.* New York: Oxford University Press.

Gumbrecht, H.U. 2004. *Production of Presence: What Meaning Cannot Convey.* Stanford: Stanford University Press.

Haber, Alejandro. 2013. Evestigation, Nomethodology, and Deictics: Movements in Un-Disciplining Archaeology in *Reclaiming Archaeology: Beyond the Tropes of Modernity.* Alfredo Gonzalez-Ruibal (Editor). London: Routledge. pp. 79-88.

Habermas, J. 1968. *Technology and Science as Ideology.*

Hacking, Ian. 1983. *Representing and Intervening: Introductory Topics in the Philosophy of Natural Science.* Cambridge: Cambridge University Press.

~John G. Sabol~

1996. Memory Science, Memory Politics in Tense Past: Cultural Essays in *Trauma and Memory.* Edited by P. Antze and M. Lambek. New York: Routledge. pp. 67-88.

Hamilakis, Yannis. 2010. Re-Collecting the Fragments: Archaeology as Mnemonic Practice in *Material Mnemonics: Everyday Memory in Prehistoric Europe.* Edited by Katina T. Lillios and Vasileios. Oxford: Oxbow. pp. 188-199.

2016. Sensorial Assemblages: Affect, Memory, and Temporality in Assemblage Thinking. *Cambridge Archaeological Journal* 27 (1): 169-182.

Hamilakis, Yannis and A. Jones. 2017. Archaeology and Assemblage. *Cambridge Archaeological Journal 27 (1): 77-84.*

Hamilakis, Yannis and Efthimis Theou. 2013. Enacted Multi-Temporality: The Archaeological Site as a Shared, Performative Space in *Reclaiming Archaeology: Beyond the Tropes of Modernity.* Edited by Alfredo Gonzalez-Ruibal. London: Routledge. pp. 181-194.

Hamilton, Paula. 1994. The Knife Edge: Debates About Memory and History in *Memory and History.* Edited by Kate Darian-Smith and Paula Hamilton. Melbourne: Oxford University Press.

Harding, Sandra. 1987. *Feminism and Methodology.* Bloomington: Indiana University Press.

Harman, Graham. 2005. *Guerrilla Metaphysics: Phenomenology and the Carpentry of Things.* Open Court.

Harrison, Rodney. 2011. Surface Assemblages: Toward an Archaeology in and of the Present. *Archaeological Dialogues* 18 (2): 141-161.

2013. Scratching the Surface: Reassembling an Archaeology in and of the Present in *Reclaiming Archaeology: Beyond the Tropes of Modernity.* Alfredo Gonzalez-Ruibal (Editor). London: Routledge. pp. 44-55.

Hayward, K. 2012. Five Spaces of Cultural Criminology. *British Journal of Criminology* 52 (3): 441-462.

Henare, Amiria, Martin Holbraad, and Sari Wastell (Editors). 2007. *Thinking Through Things: Theorising Artefacts Ethnographically.* London: Routledge.

Herva, Vesa-Pekka. 2014. Haunting Heritage in an Enchanted Land: Magic, Materiality and Second World War German Material Heritage in Finnish Lapland. *Journal of Contemporary Archaeology* 1 (2): 297-321.

Herzfeld, Michael. 2012. Whose Rights to Which Past? Archaeologists, Anthropologists, and the Ethics and Aesthetics of Heritage in the Global Hierarchy of Value in *Archaeology and Anthropology: Past, present, and Future.* Edited by David Shankland. London: Bloomsburg. pp. 41-64.

Hewison, R. 1989. Heritage: An Interpretation in *Heritage Interpretation.* D.L. Uzell (Editor). London: Belhaven Press. pp. 15-23.

Holdorf, Cornelius. 2017. On Pastness: A Reconsideration of Materiality in Archaeological Object Authenticity. *Anthropological Quarterly* 86: 427-444.

Holmberg, Karen. 2013. The Sound of Sulphur and Smell of Lightning: Sensing the Volcano in *Making Senses of the Past: Toward a Sensory Archaeology.* Edited by Jo Day. Carbondale: Southern Illinois University Press. pp. 49-68.

Hudson, Mark James. 2014. Dark Artifacts: Hyperobjects, and the Archaeology of the Anthropocene. *Journal of Contemporary Archaeology* 1 (1): 82-86.

Ingold, Tim. 1993. The Temporality of the Landscape. *World Archaeology* 25 (2): 152-174.

Kern, Stephen. 1983. *The Culture of Time and Space 1880-1918.* Cambridge: Blackwell.

Kim-Cohen, S. 2009. *In the Blink of an Ear: Toward a Non_Cochlear Sound Art.* New York: Continuum.

Kubler, George. 1962. *The Shape of Time: Remarks on the History of Things.* Yale University Press.

Kuchler, Susan. 1993. Colonialism, History, and the Construction of Place: The Politics of Landscape in Northern Australia in *Landscape: Politics and Perspectives.* Barbara Bender (Editor), Oxford: Berg. pp. 205-243.

Laidlaw, James. 1994. The Archtypal Actions of Ritual: A Theory of Ritual Illustrated by the Jain Rite of Worship. *Oxford: Clarendon Press.*

Lefebvre, Henri. 2004. *Rhythmnanalysis: Space, Time and Everyday Life.* Translation: Stuart Elden and Gerald Moore. London: Bloomsbury Academic.

Leroi-Gourhan, Andre. 1950. Les Fouilles Prehistoriques (Techniques et Methodes). Paris: A et J. Picard.

Lim, Bliss Cua. 2009. *Translating Time: Cinema, the Fantastic, and Temporal Critique.* Durham, North Carolina: Duke University Press.

Lucas, Gavin. 2001. *Critical Approaches to Fieldwork: Contemporary and Historical Archaeological Practice.* London: Routledge.

Mali, Joseph. 2003. *Mythistory: The Making of a Modern Historiography.* Chicago: University of Chicago Press.

Manning, Paul. 2017. No Ruins, No Ghosts. *Preternature: Critical and Historical Studies on the Preternatural* Volume 6 (1): 63-92. State College: Penn State University Press.

Massey, D. 1994. Landscape as a Provocation: Reflections on Moving Mountains. *Journal of Material Culture* 11: 33-48.

2006. Landscape as a Practice: Reflections on Moving Mountains. *Journal of Material Culture 11: 33-48.*

McCombe, Christine. 2001. Imagining Space Through Sound in Sound Practice Proceedings, University of Edinburgh. The First UKISK Conference on Sound, Culture, and Environments.

McNiven, Ian. 2013. Between the Living and the Dead: Relational Ontology and the Ritual Dimensions of Dugong Hunting Across Torres Strait in *Relational Archaeologies: Humans, Animals, Things.* Edited by Christopher Watts. London: Routledge.

Morphy, Howard. 1993. Landscape as Memory: The Mapping of Process and its Representation in a Melanesian Society in *Landscape: Politics and Perspectives.* Barbara Bender (Editor). Oxford: Berg. pp. 85-106.

Moshenska, G. 2013. The Archaeological Gaze in *Reclaiming Archaeology: Beyond the Tropes of Modernity.* Edited by Alfredo Gonzalez-Ruibal. London: Routledge. pp. 211-219.

Moshenska, G. and T. Schadla-Hall. 2011. Mortimer Wheeler's Theatre of the Past. *Public Archaeology* 10 (1): 46-55.

Oakeshott, Michael. 1933. *Experience and its Modes.* Cambridge: Cambridge University Press.

Olivier, Laurent. 2001. The Archaeology of the Contemporary Past in *Archaeologies of the Contemporary Past.* V. Buchli and G. Lucas (Editors). London: Routledge. pp. 175-188.

2008/2011. *The Dark Abyss of Time: Archaeology and Memory.* Lanham (Maryland): AltaMira Press.

Olsen, B. Michael Shanks, T. Webmoor, C. Witmore. 2012. *Archaeology: The Discipline of Things.* Berkeley: University of California Press.

Ondaatje, Michael. 2000. *Anil's Ghost.* New York: Alfred A. Knopf.

Pearson, Mike and Michael Shanks. 2001. *Theatre/Archaeology.* London: Routledge.

Peters, Gary. 2009. *The Philosophy of Improvisation.* Chicago: University of Chicago Press.

Petersson, Bodil and Lars Erik Narmo. 2011 (Editors). Experimental Archaeology: Between Enlightenment and Experience. *Lund Acta Archaeologica Lundensia Series 8 (Volume 62).* Lund: Lund University of Archaeology and Ancient History.

Petursdottir, Dora, and Bjornar Olsen. 2017. Theory Adrift: The Matter of Archaeological Theorizing. *Journal of Social Archaeology* pp. 1-21.

Proctor, J. 2002. Late Bronze Age/Early Iron Age Placed Deposits from Westcroft Road, Casrshalton: Their Meaning and Interpretation. *Surrey Archaeological Collections* 89: 65-103.

Renfrew, Colin and Bahn. 2008. Archaeology and Assemblage. *Archaeological Journal 27 (1): 77-84.*

Robb, J. 2010. Beyond Agency. *World Archaeology* 42 (4): 493-520.

Russell, Ian. 2006. Images of the Past: Archaeologies, Modernities, Crises, and Poetics in *Images, Representations, and Heritage: Moving Beyond Modern*

Approaches to Archaeology. Ian Russell (Editor). New York: Springer. pp. 1-38.

Santos-Granero, F. (Editor). 2009. *The Occult Life iof Things: Native Amazonian Theories of Materiality and Personhood.* Tucson: University of Arizona Press.

Schiffer, Michael. 1976. *Behavioral Archaeology.* London: Academic Press.

1987. *Formation Processes of the Archaeological Record.* Albuquerque: University of New Mexico Press.

Schlanger, S. 1992. Recognizing Persistent Places in Anasazi Settlement Systems in *Space, Time, and Archaeological Landscape.* Edited by J. Rossignol and L. Wandsnider. New York: Plenum Press. pp. 91-112.

Schneider, Rebecca. 2011. *Performing Remains: Art and War in Times of Theatrical Reenactment.* London: Routledge.

2014. *Theatre and History.* New York: St. Martin's Press.

Schofield, John. 2011. Greatness in Depth: Why Excavations Matter in *Great Excavations: Shaping the Archaeological Profession.* John Schofield (Editor). Oxford: Oxbow. pp. 1-11.

Seremetakis, C. N. 1996. The Memory of the Senses: Part 1-Marks of the Transitory in *The Senses Still: Perception and*

Memory as Material Culture in Modernity. C. N. Seremetakis (Editor). Chicago: Chicago University Press.

Shanks, Michael. 1991/1992. *Experiencing the Past: On the Character of Archaeology.* London: Routledge.

2012. *The Archaeological Imagination.* Walnut Creek, California: Left Coast Press.

Shennan, S. 1993. After Social Evolution: A New Archaeological Agenda? In *Archaeological Theory: Who Sets the Agenda?* Edited by N. Yoffee and A. Sherratt. Cambridge: Cambridge University Press. pp. 53-59.

Shepherd, Nick. 2007. Archaeological Dreaming: Post-Apartheid Urban Imaginaries and the Bones of the Prestwich Street Dead. *Journal of Social Archaeology.* 7 (1): 3-28.

Silliman, Stephen (Editor). 2018. Engaging Archaeology: An Introduction and a Guide in *Engaging Archaeology: 25 Case Studies in Research Practice.* Hoboken, New Jersey: John Wiley and Sons, Inc. pp. 1-11.

Sloterdijks, Peter. 1999. *SpharenII: Globen.* Frankfurt am Main: Sumrkamp.

Smith, M.A. 1955. The Limitations of Inference in Archaeology. *Archaeological Newsletter* 6:3-7. Paper read at the Conference of the Prehistoric Society, University of London (Institute of Archaeology).

~John G. Sabol~

Sobin, Gustaf. 1999. *Luminous Debris.* Berkeley: University of California Press.

Stallworthy, John. 1982. W.B. Yeats and Seamus Heaney: The Poet as Archaeologist in *Review of English Studies* Volume 33 (No. 130): 158-174.

Starzmann, Maria Theresia. 2016. Engaging Memory: An Introduction in *Excavating Memory: Sites of Remembering and Forgetting.* Maria Theresia Starzmann and John R. Roby (Editors). Gainesville: University Press of Florida. pp. 1-24.

Stewart, K. 2011. Atmospheric Attunements. *Environment and Planning D: Society and Space* 29 (3): 445-453.

Stoler, Ann Laura. 2013. (Editor) *Imperial Debris: On Ruins and Ruination.* Durham: Duke University Press.

Strathern, Andrew. 1993. *Landmarks: Reflections on Anthropology.* Kent, Ohio: The Kent State University Press.

Sumyer Yu, Dan. 2015. Mindscaping the Landscape of Tibet: Place, Memorability, Ecoaesthetics in *Religion and Society Volume 60.* Edited by G. Benavides, K. von Stucjrad, W. Fallers Sullivan. Boston: Walter de Gruyter, Inc.

Taussig, Michael. 1987. *Shamanism, Colonialism, and the Wild Man: A Study in Terror and Healing.* Chicago: University of Chicago Press.

Thomas, Julian. 1996. *Time, Culture, and Identity: An Interpretive Archaeology.* London: Routledge.

Thrush, Coll. 2011. Hauntings as Histories: Indigenous Ghosts and the Urban Past in Seattle in *Phantom Past, Indigenous Present: North American Ghosts in Native American Culture and History.* Edited by Colleen E. Boyd and Coll Thrush. Lincoln: University of Nebraska Press. pp. 54-81.

Tilden, Freeman. 1957. *Interpreting our Heritage.* Chapel Hill: University of North Carolina Press.

Tilley, Christopher. 1989. Excavation as Theatre. *Antiquity* 63: 275-280.

1994. *A Phenomenology of Landscape: Places, Paths, and Monuments.* Oxford: Berg.

2011. Materializing Identities: An Introduction. *Journal of Material Culture* 16 (4): 347-357.

Toop, David. 2010. *Sinister Resonance.* London: The Continuum Publishing Group, Ltd.

Vergunst, J. 2012. Spectral Geographies: Haunting and Everyday State Practices in Colonial and Present-Day Alaska. *Social and Cultural Geography* 12 (7): 743-756.

Vivieros de Castro, Eduardo. 1998. Cosmological Deixis and Ameridian Perspectivism. *Journal of the Royal Anthropological Institute Volume 4 (3): 469-488.*

Wallace, Jennifer. 2004. *Digging the Dirt: The Archaeological Imagination.* London: Gerald Duckworth & Company, Ltd.

Watts, Christopher. 2013. *Relational Archaeologies: Humans, Animals, Things.* Edited by Christopher Watts. London: Routledge.

Weismantle, Mary. 2015. Looking Like an Archaeologist: Viveiros de Castro at Chavin de Huantar. *Journal of Social Archaeology* 15 (3): 139-159.

Wheeler, Sir Mortimer. 1954. *Archaeology from the Earth.* Harmondsworth: Penguin.

Willerslev, Rene. 2007. *Soul Hunters: Hunting, Animism, and Personhood Among the Siberian Yukaghirs.* Berkeley: University of California Press.

Witmore, Christopher. 2014. Archaeology and the New Materialisms. *Journal of Contemporary Archaeology* 1 (2): 203-246.

2017. Things are the Grounds of All Archaeology: Notes on the Arvanitia Xenia in *Clashes of Time: The Contemporary Past as a Challenge to Archaeology.* Edited by Jean-Marie Blaising, Jan Driessen, Jean-Pierre Legendre, Laurent Olivier. Louvain-la-Neuve, Belgium: Presses Universitaires de Louvain. pp. 231-232.Wood, Andy. 2013. *The Memory of the People: Custom and Popular Senses in Early Modern England.* Cambridge: Cambridge University Press.

Woodward, Christopher. 2001. *In Ruins: A Journey Through History, Art, and Literature.* New York: Vintage.

Yentsch, Anne. 1988. Legends, Houses, Families, and Myths: Relationships between Material Culture and

~John G. Sabol~

Past Immiscible:
Digging into Uncommon Ground

American Ideology in *Documentary Archaeology in the New World*. Edited by Mary C. Beaudry. Cambridge: Cambridge University Press. pp. 5-19.

~John G. Sabol~

About the Author

John Sabol is an archaeologist, cultural anthropologist, actor, and author. As an archaeologist, he has unearthed past material remains in excavations and site surveys in England, Mexico, and at various sites in the United States (including Eastern South Dakota, the Tennessee River Valleys, and in Pennsylvania). His anthropological fieldwork includes the studies of "spirits" in the religious beliefs of the afterlife among various cultural groups in Mexico (Mixtec, Zapotec, Lacandon, Nahuatl, and Otomi). His acting career includes "ghosting" performances of various characters and scenarios in more than 35 movies, TV shows, and documentaries. He has appeared in the A&E TV series, Paranormal State as an investigative consultant. He has written over thirty books.

His recent speaking engagements include the T.A.G. (Theoretical Archaeology Group) Conference at the University of California, Berkeley, at the Space and Place Conference in Prague, Czech Republic, the TAG Conference at the University in Buffalo, New York, Exploring the Extraordinary Conference in York, England, the C.H.A.T. archaeological conference also in York, and the GHost Conference at the University of London, London, England.

His investigative reports have been published in such diverse venues as Haunted Times Magazine, Tennessee Anthropologist, and the online journal, ParaAnthropology. He has been a frequent guest on numerous radio and

~John G. Sabol~

internet talk shows, among them, Beyond the Edge Radio, The Paranormal View, Para X Radio, Blog Talk Radio, The Grand Dark Conspiracy, and Rusty O'Nhiall's "Mysterious and Unexplained" on PsiFM (Australia). He was a university professor in Mexico for 11 years, teaching both undergraduate and graduate courses on the anthropology of tourism. He has also been featured on public educational TV for U.S. and foreign markets, and has worked on international educational documentaries (in Spain).

He has a M.A. in Anthropology/Archaeology (University of Tennessee), and a B.A. in Sociology/Anthropology (Bloomsburg University). He has also attended Penn State University, the University of Pittsburgh, the University of the Americas (Cholula, Puebla, Mexico), and has studied theatre and method acting in Mexico City.

He can be reached via email at cuicospirit@hotmail.com. His website is: **www.ghostexcavation.com** and he can be found on Facebook, *Ghost Excavations with John Sabol*.

~John G. Sabol~